COOL CARS

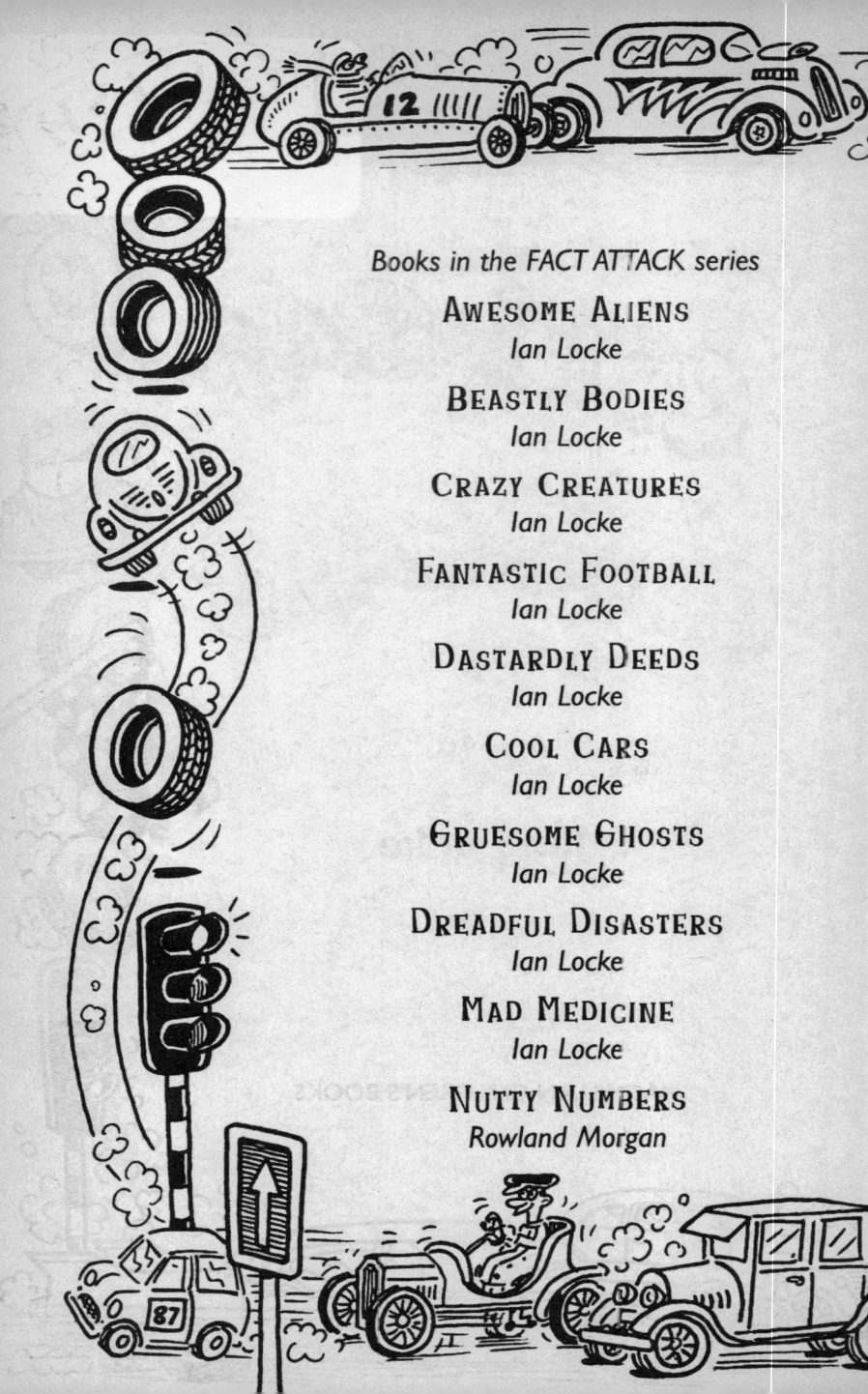

Books in the *FACT ATTACK* series

AWESOME ALIENS
Ian Locke

BEASTLY BODIES
Ian Locke

CRAZY CREATURES
Ian Locke

FANTASTIC FOOTBALL
Ian Locke

DASTARDLY DEEDS
Ian Locke

COOL CARS
Ian Locke

GRUESOME GHOSTS
Ian Locke

DREADFUL DISASTERS
Ian Locke

MAD MEDICINE
Ian Locke

NUTTY NUMBERS
Rowland Morgan

FACT ATTACK

COOL CARS

Ian Locke

MACMILLAN CHILDREN'S BOOKS

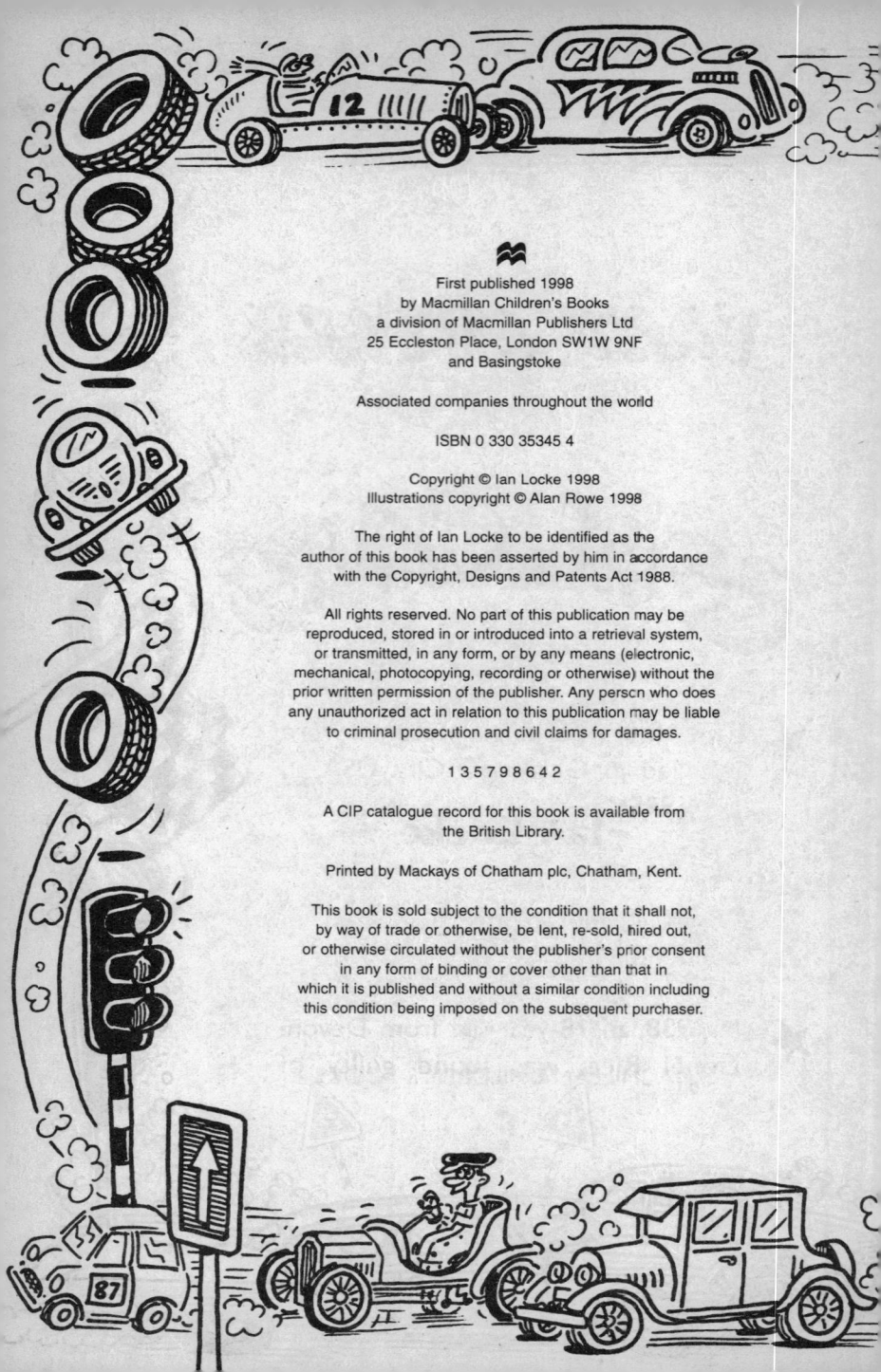

First published 1998
by Macmillan Children's Books
a division of Macmillan Publishers Ltd
25 Eccleston Place, London SW1W 9NF
and Basingstoke

Associated companies throughout the world

ISBN 0 330 35345 4

Copyright © Ian Locke 1998
Illustrations copyright © Alan Rowe 1998

The right of Ian Locke to be identified as the
author of this book has been asserted by him in accordance
with the Copyright, Designs and Patents Act 1988.

1 3 5 7 9 8 6 4 2

A CIP catalogue record for this book is available from
the British Library.

Printed by Mackays of Chatham plc, Chatham, Kent.

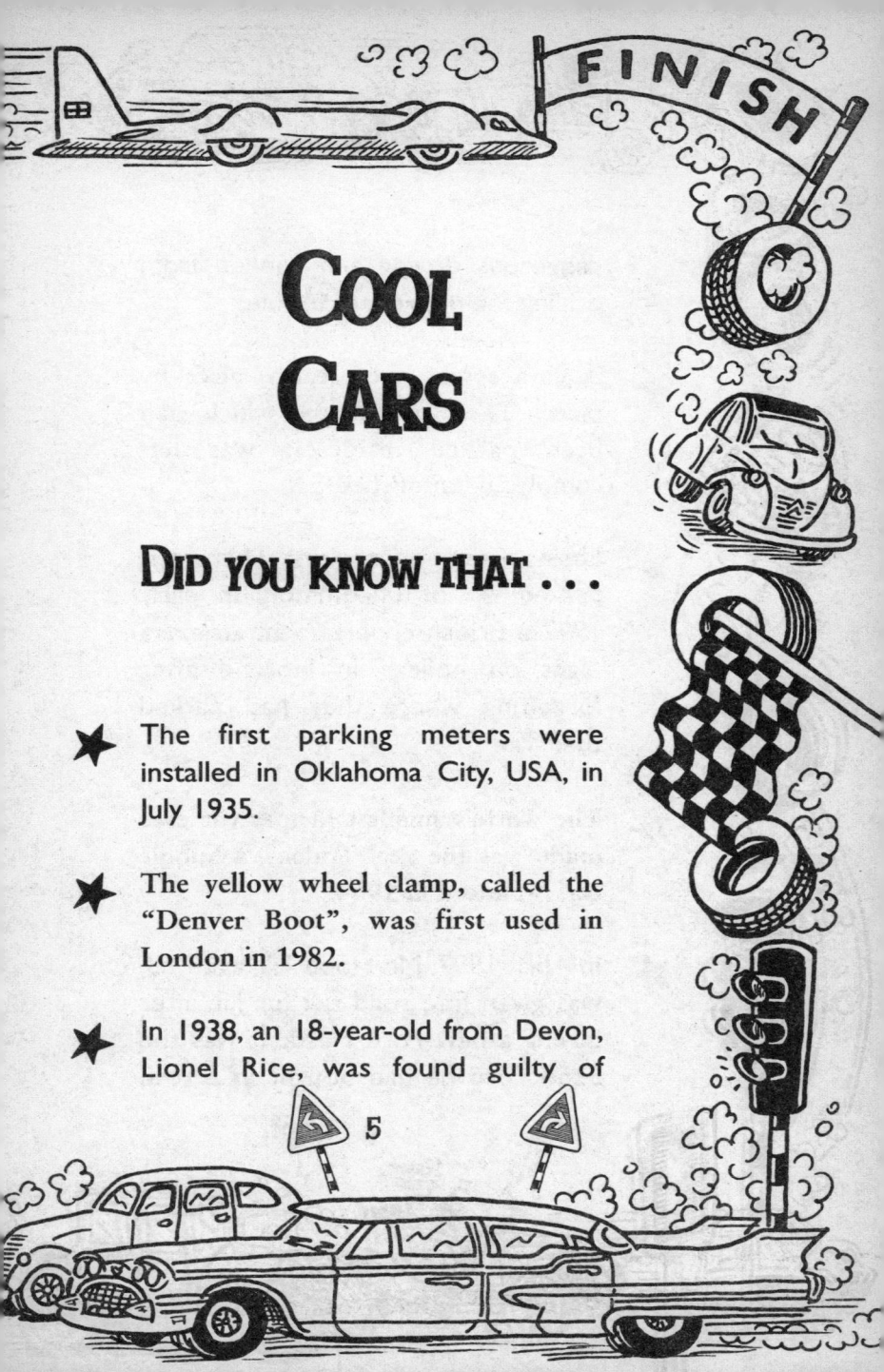

COOL CARS

DID YOU KNOW THAT . . .

★ The first parking meters were installed in Oklahoma City, USA, in July 1935.

★ The yellow wheel clamp, called the "Denver Boot", was first used in London in 1982.

★ In 1938, an 18-year-old from Devon, Lionel Rice, was found guilty of

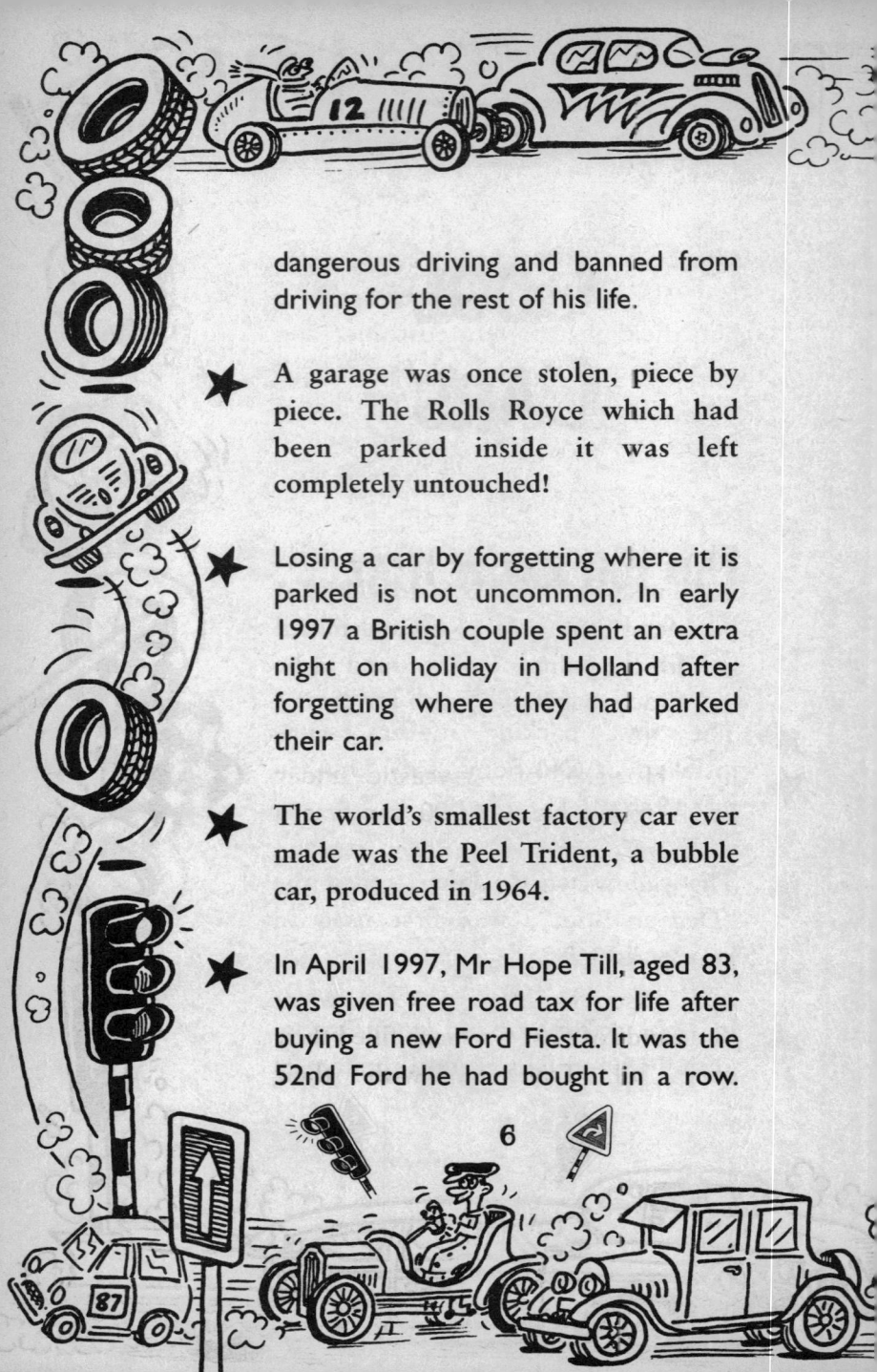

dangerous driving and banned from driving for the rest of his life.

★ A garage was once stolen, piece by piece. The Rolls Royce which had been parked inside it was left completely untouched!

★ Losing a car by forgetting where it is parked is not uncommon. In early 1997 a British couple spent an extra night on holiday in Holland after forgetting where they had parked their car.

★ The world's smallest factory car ever made was the Peel Trident, a bubble car, produced in 1964.

★ In April 1997, Mr Hope Till, aged 83, was given free road tax for life after buying a new Ford Fiesta. It was the 52nd Ford he had bought in a row.

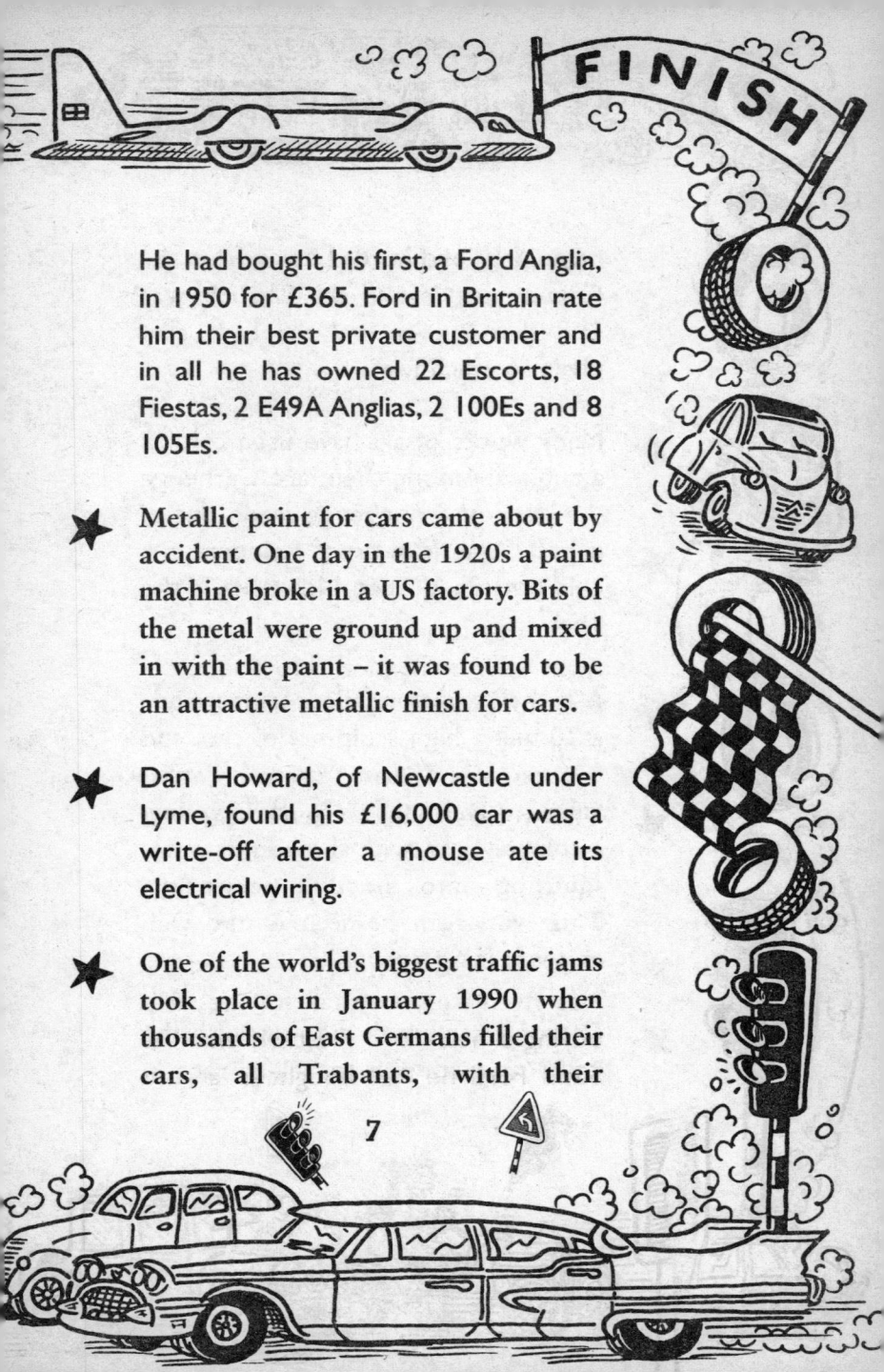

He had bought his first, a Ford Anglia, in 1950 for £365. Ford in Britain rate him their best private customer and in all he has owned 22 Escorts, 18 Fiestas, 2 E49A Anglias, 2 100Es and 8 105Es.

★ Metallic paint for cars came about by accident. One day in the 1920s a paint machine broke in a US factory. Bits of the metal were ground up and mixed in with the paint – it was found to be an attractive metallic finish for cars.

★ Dan Howard, of Newcastle under Lyme, found his £16,000 car was a write-off after a mouse ate its electrical wiring.

★ One of the world's biggest traffic jams took place in January 1990 when thousands of East Germans filled their cars, all Trabants, with their

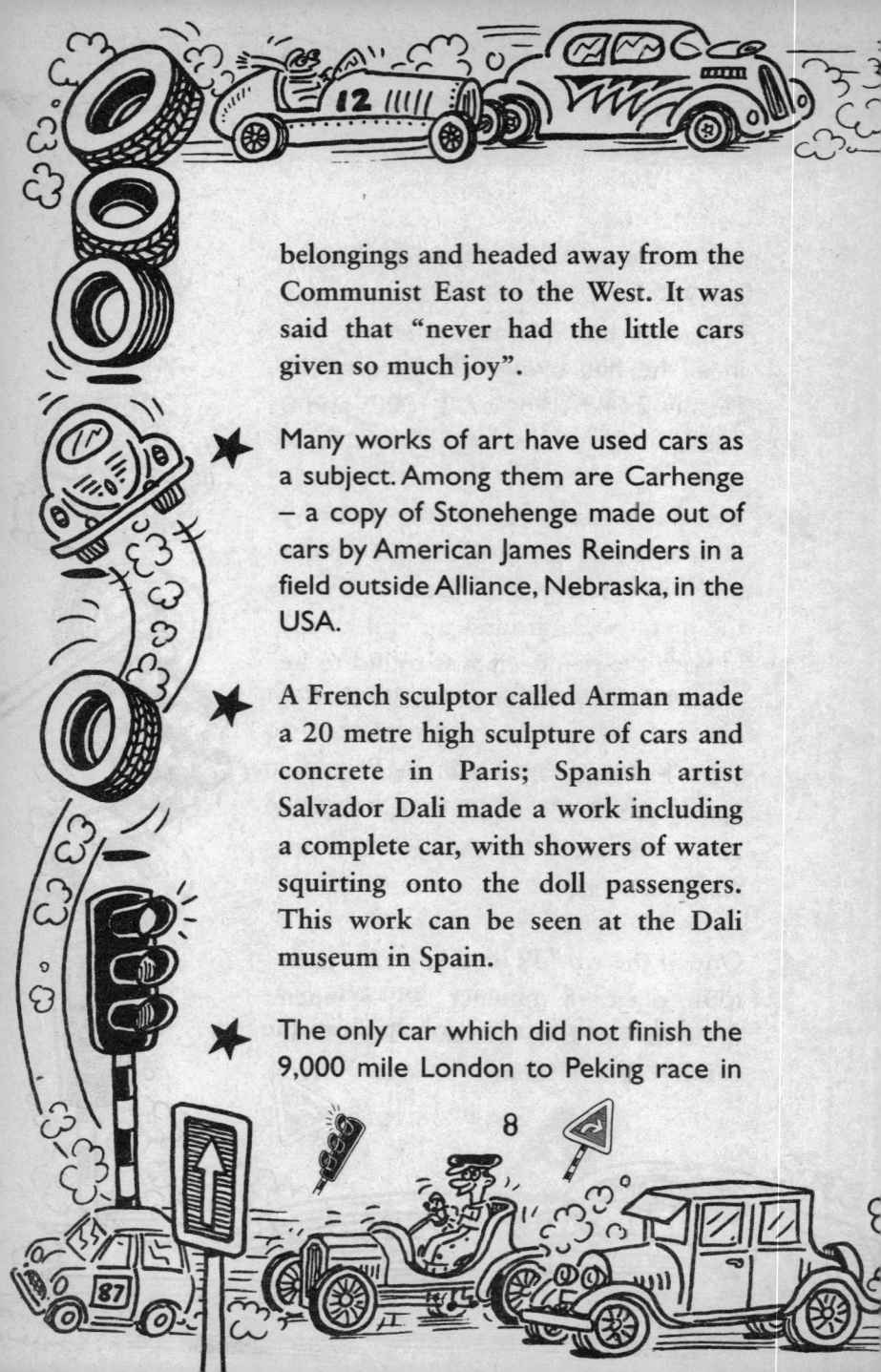

belongings and headed away from the Communist East to the West. It was said that "never had the little cars given so much joy".

★ Many works of art have used cars as a subject. Among them are Carhenge – a copy of Stonehenge made out of cars by American James Reinders in a field outside Alliance, Nebraska, in the USA.

★ A French sculptor called Arman made a 20 metre high sculpture of cars and concrete in Paris; Spanish artist Salvador Dali made a work including a complete car, with showers of water squirting onto the doll passengers. This work can be seen at the Dali museum in Spain.

★ The only car which did not finish the 9,000 mile London to Peking race in

8

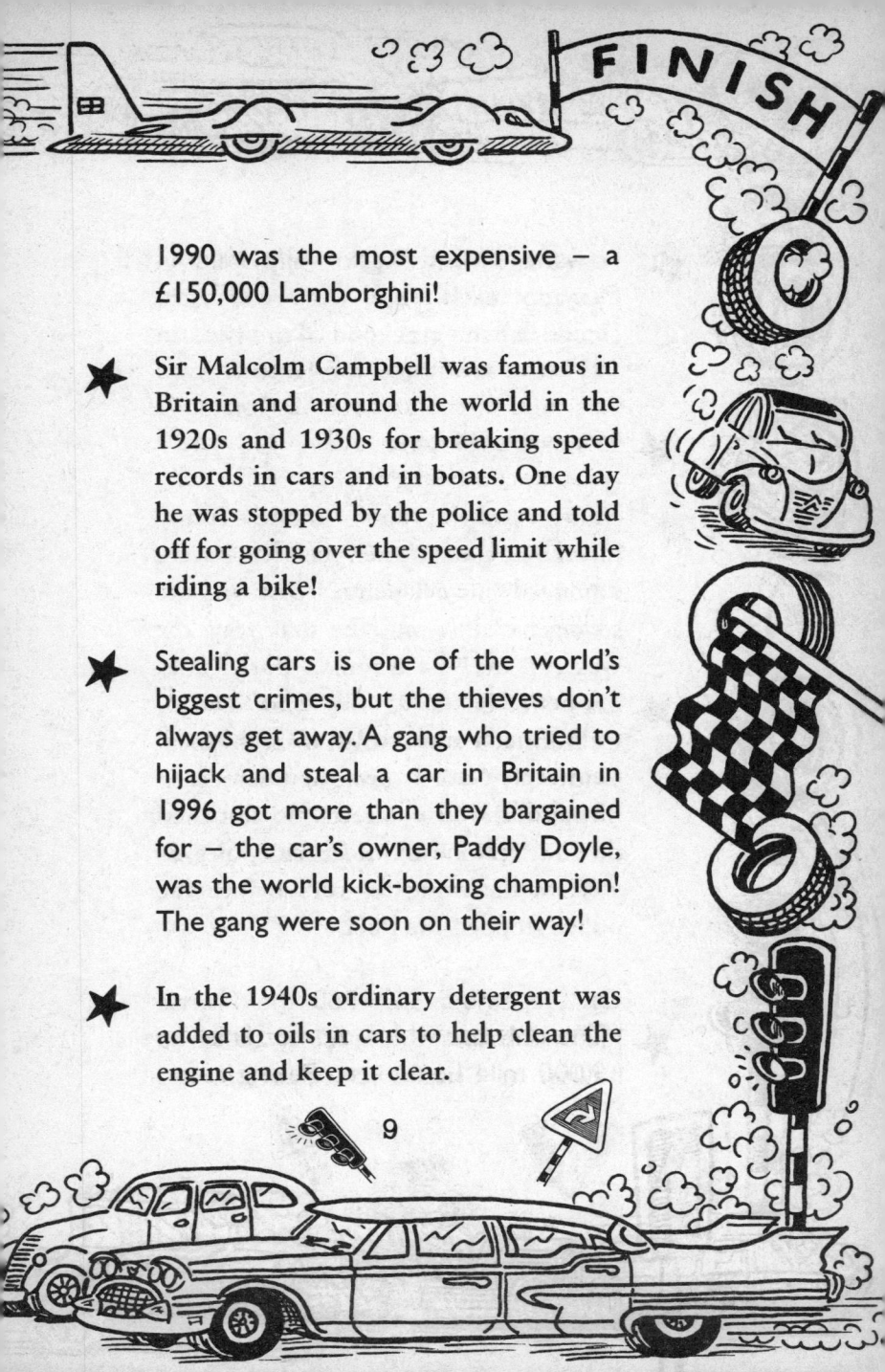

1990 was the most expensive – a £150,000 Lamborghini!

★ Sir Malcolm Campbell was famous in Britain and around the world in the 1920s and 1930s for breaking speed records in cars and in boats. One day he was stopped by the police and told off for going over the speed limit while riding a bike!

★ Stealing cars is one of the world's biggest crimes, but the thieves don't always get away. A gang who tried to hijack and steal a car in Britain in 1996 got more than they bargained for – the car's owner, Paddy Doyle, was the world kick-boxing champion! The gang were soon on their way!

★ In the 1940s ordinary detergent was added to oils in cars to help clean the engine and keep it clear.

9

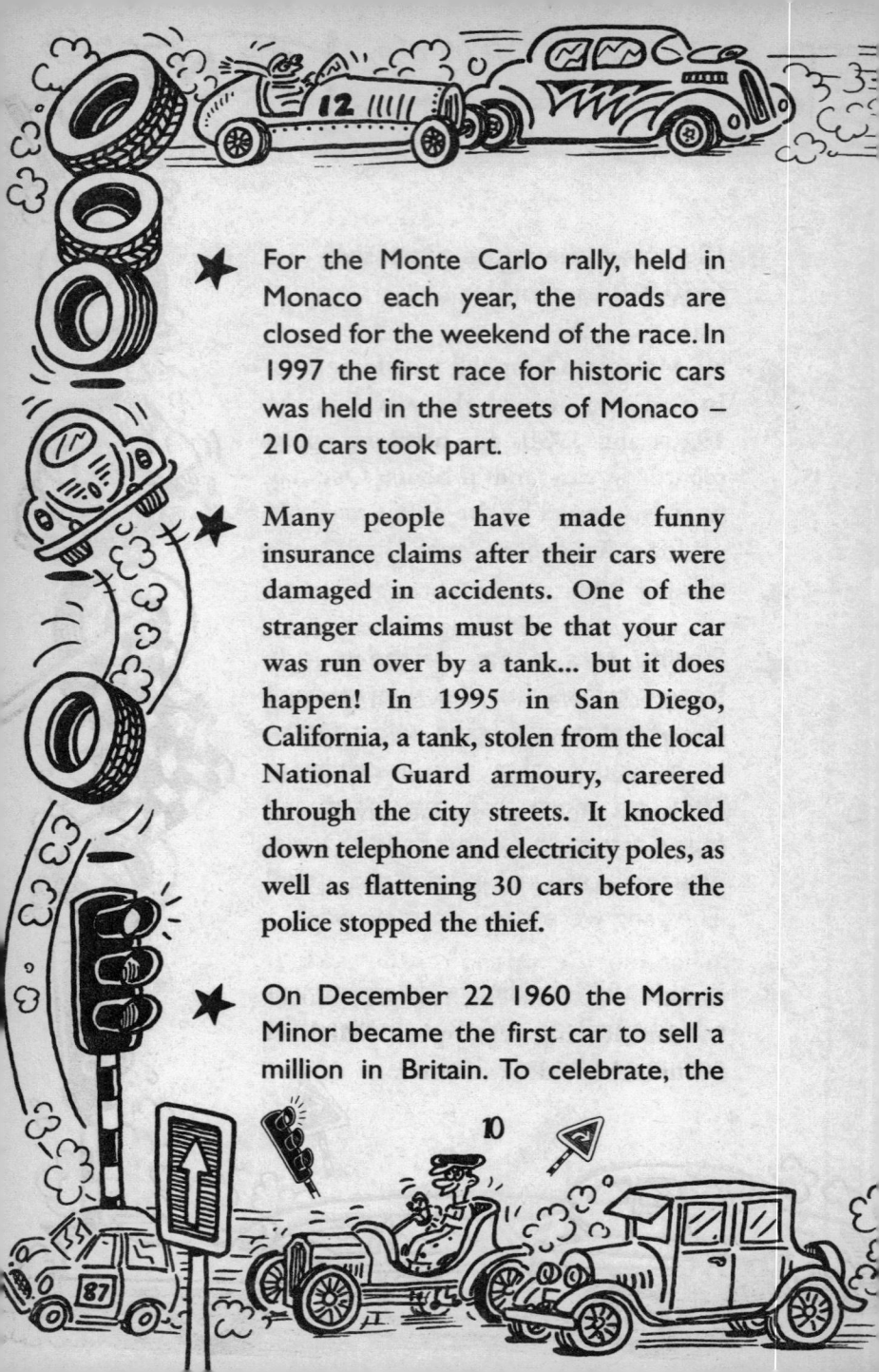

For the Monte Carlo rally, held in Monaco each year, the roads are closed for the weekend of the race. In 1997 the first race for historic cars was held in the streets of Monaco – 210 cars took part.

Many people have made funny insurance claims after their cars were damaged in accidents. One of the stranger claims must be that your car was run over by a tank... but it does happen! In 1995 in San Diego, California, a tank, stolen from the local National Guard armoury, careered through the city streets. It knocked down telephone and electricity poles, as well as flattening 30 cars before the police stopped the thief.

On December 22 1960 the Morris Minor became the first car to sell a million in Britain. To celebrate, the

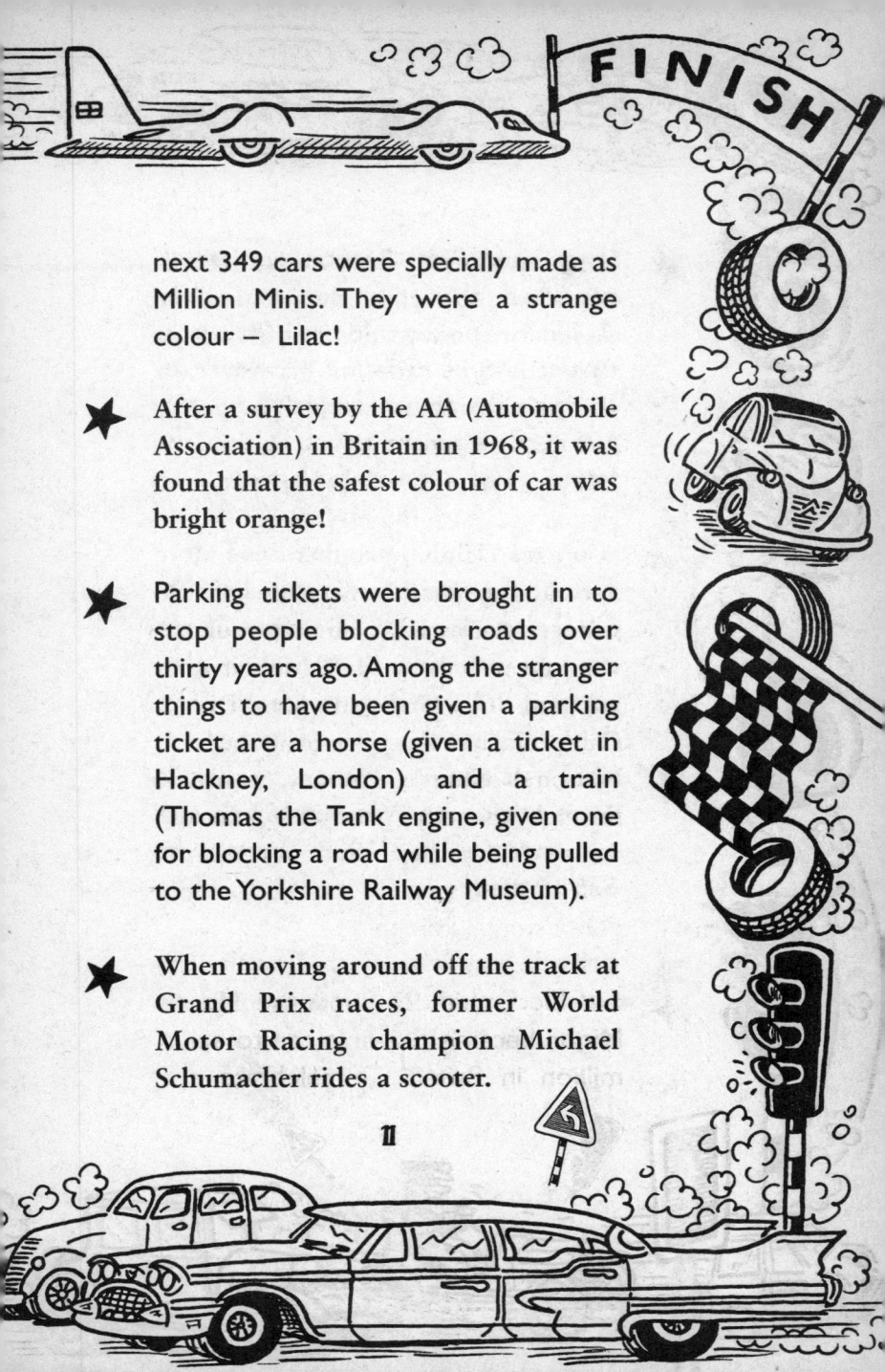

next 349 cars were specially made as Million Minis. They were a strange colour – Lilac!

★ After a survey by the AA (Automobile Association) in Britain in 1968, it was found that the safest colour of car was bright orange!

★ Parking tickets were brought in to stop people blocking roads over thirty years ago. Among the stranger things to have been given a parking ticket are a horse (given a ticket in Hackney, London) and a train (Thomas the Tank engine, given one for blocking a road while being pulled to the Yorkshire Railway Museum).

★ When moving around off the track at Grand Prix races, former World Motor Racing champion Michael Schumacher rides a scooter.

11

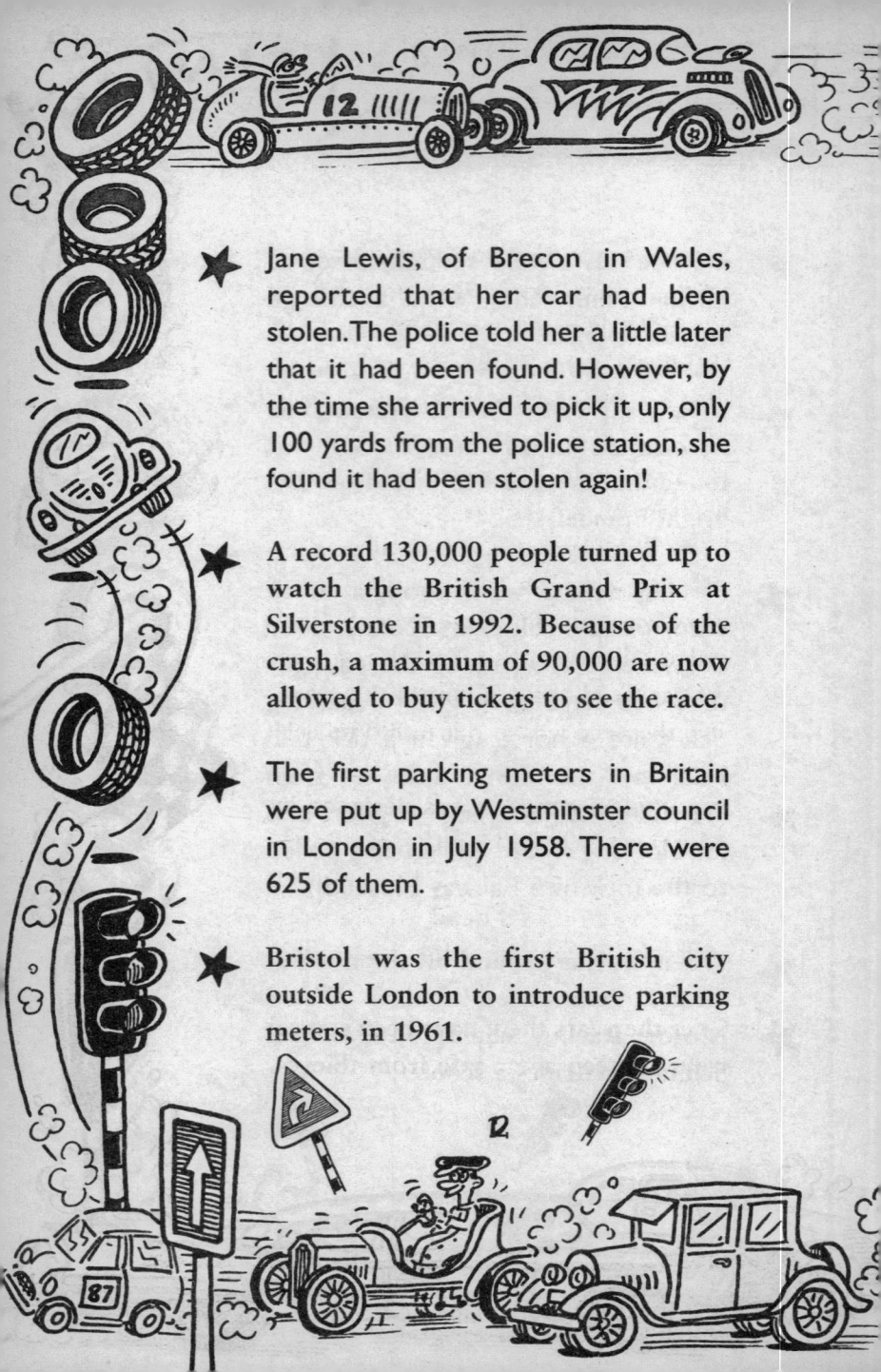

★ Jane Lewis, of Brecon in Wales, reported that her car had been stolen. The police told her a little later that it had been found. However, by the time she arrived to pick it up, only 100 yards from the police station, she found it had been stolen again!

★ A record 130,000 people turned up to watch the British Grand Prix at Silverstone in 1992. Because of the crush, a maximum of 90,000 are now allowed to buy tickets to see the race.

★ The first parking meters in Britain were put up by Westminster council in London in July 1958. There were 625 of them.

★ Bristol was the first British city outside London to introduce parking meters, in 1961.

12

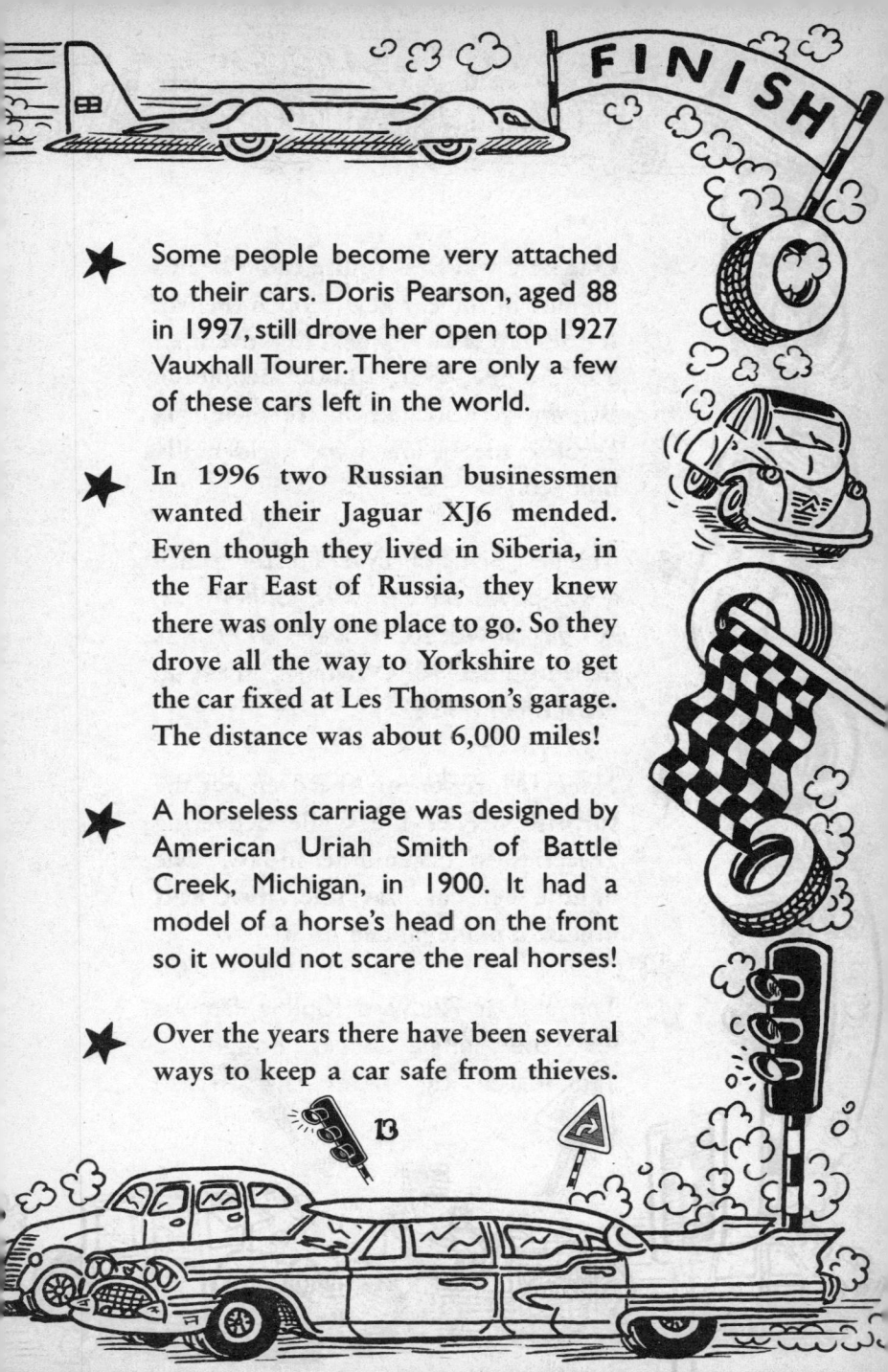

★ Some people become very attached to their cars. Doris Pearson, aged 88 in 1997, still drove her open top 1927 Vauxhall Tourer. There are only a few of these cars left in the world.

★ In 1996 two Russian businessmen wanted their Jaguar XJ6 mended. Even though they lived in Siberia, in the Far East of Russia, they knew there was only one place to go. So they drove all the way to Yorkshire to get the car fixed at Les Thomson's garage. The distance was about 6,000 miles!

★ A horseless carriage was designed by American Uriah Smith of Battle Creek, Michigan, in 1900. It had a model of a horse's head on the front so it would not scare the real horses!

★ Over the years there have been several ways to keep a car safe from thieves.

13

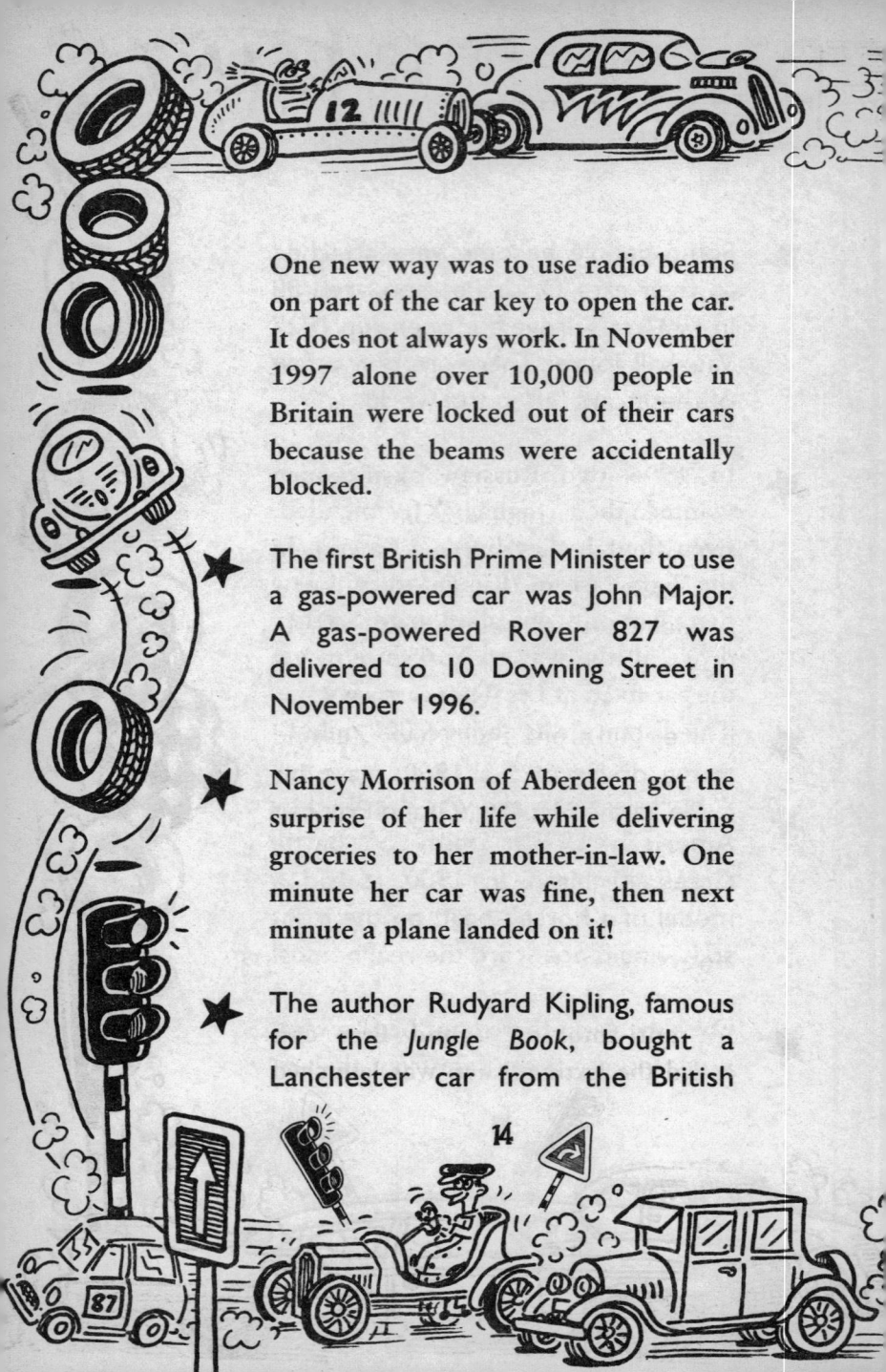

One new way was to use radio beams on part of the car key to open the car. It does not always work. In November 1997 alone over 10,000 people in Britain were locked out of their cars because the beams were accidentally blocked.

★ The first British Prime Minister to use a gas-powered car was John Major. A gas-powered Rover 827 was delivered to 10 Downing Street in November 1996.

★ Nancy Morrison of Aberdeen got the surprise of her life while delivering groceries to her mother-in-law. One minute her car was fine, then next minute a plane landed on it!

★ The author Rudyard Kipling, famous for the *Jungle Book*, bought a Lanchester car from the British

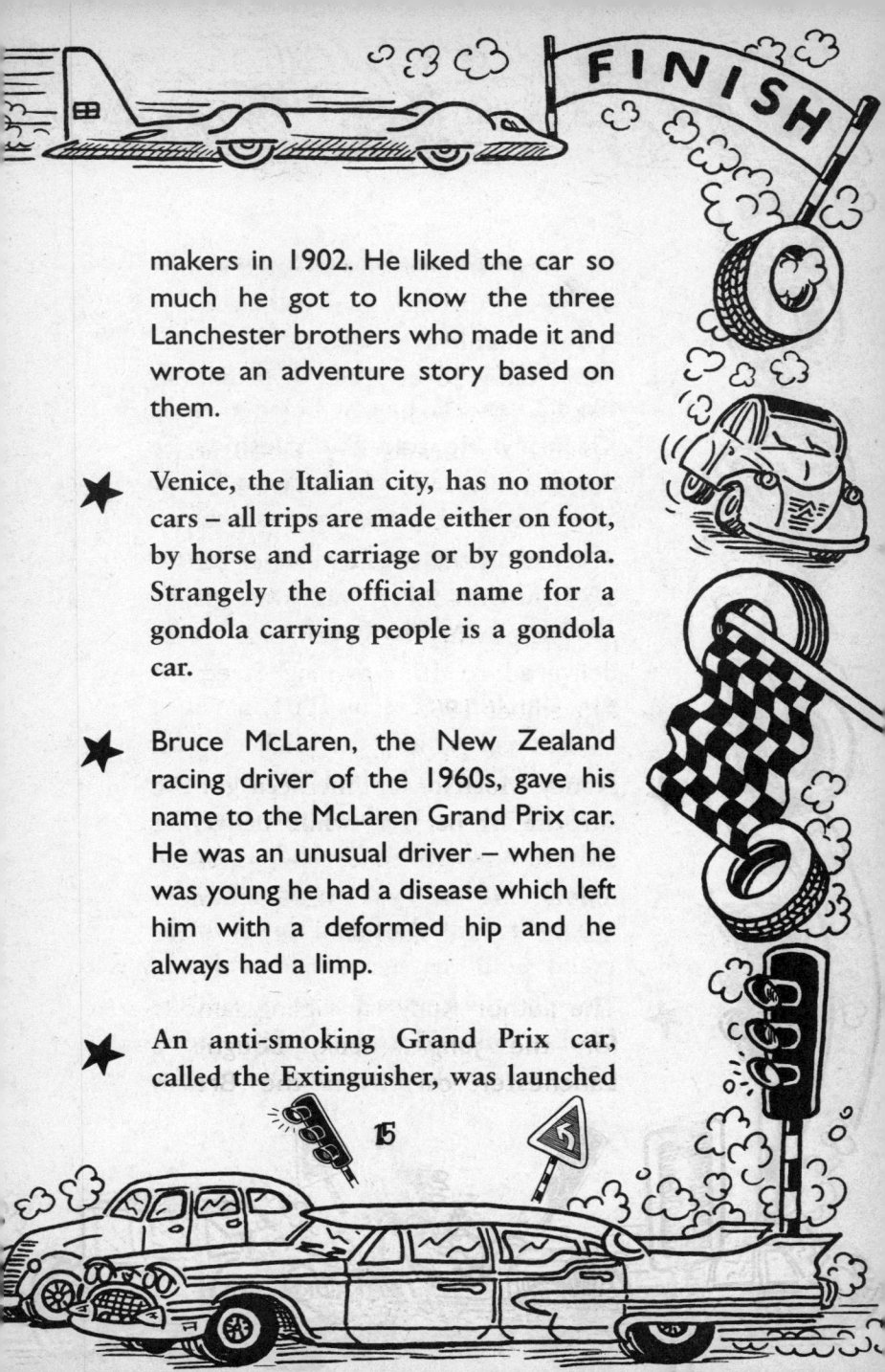

makers in 1902. He liked the car so much he got to know the three Lanchester brothers who made it and wrote an adventure story based on them.

★ Venice, the Italian city, has no motor cars – all trips are made either on foot, by horse and carriage or by gondola. Strangely the official name for a gondola carrying people is a gondola car.

★ Bruce McLaren, the New Zealand racing driver of the 1960s, gave his name to the McLaren Grand Prix car. He was an unusual driver – when he was young he had a disease which left him with a deformed hip and he always had a limp.

★ An anti-smoking Grand Prix car, called the Extinguisher, was launched

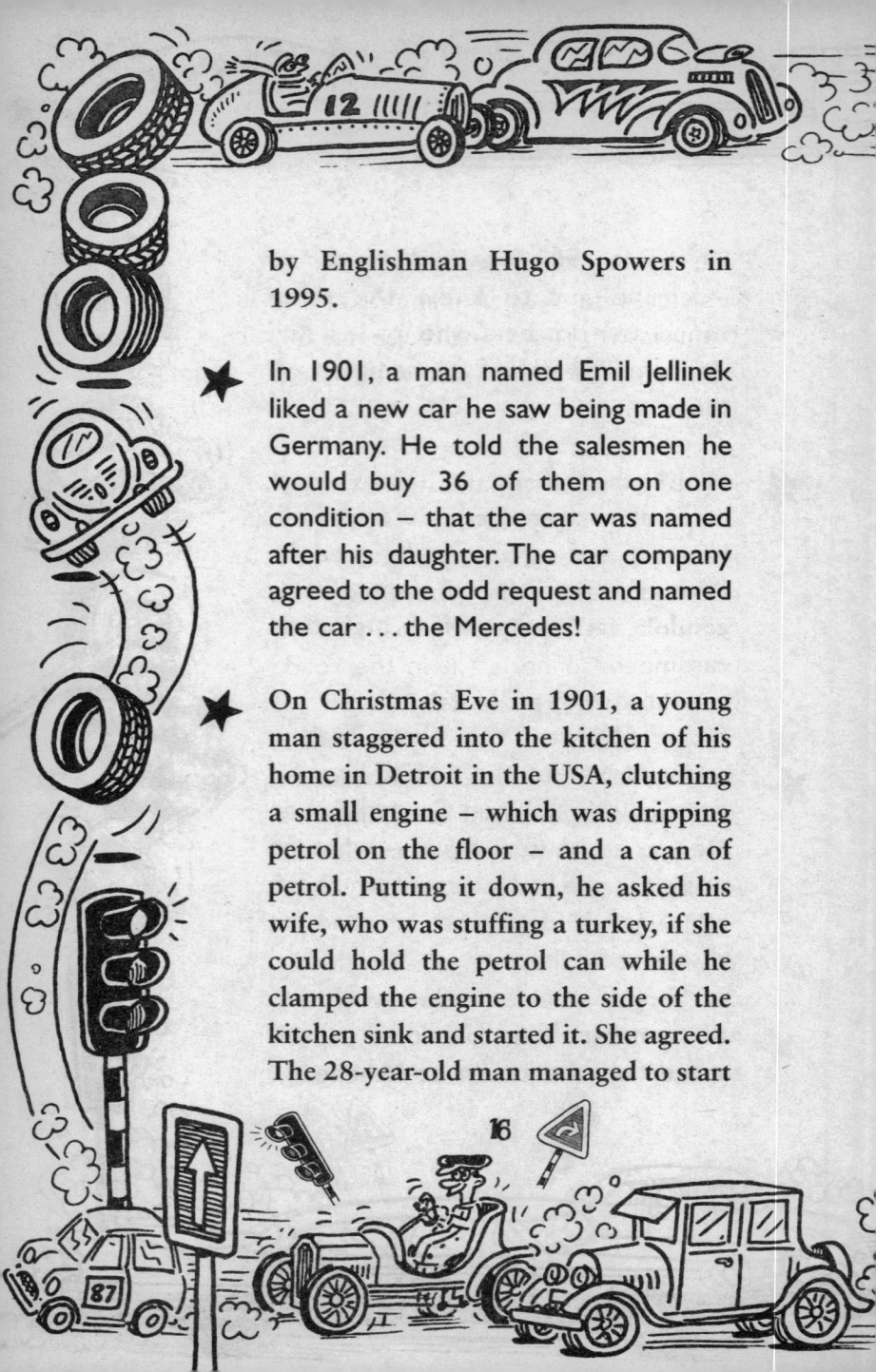

by Englishman Hugo Spowers in 1995.

★ In 1901, a man named Emil Jellinek liked a new car he saw being made in Germany. He told the salesmen he would buy 36 of them on one condition – that the car was named after his daughter. The car company agreed to the odd request and named the car ... the Mercedes!

★ On Christmas Eve in 1901, a young man staggered into the kitchen of his home in Detroit in the USA, clutching a small engine – which was dripping petrol on the floor – and a can of petrol. Putting it down, he asked his wife, who was stuffing a turkey, if she could hold the petrol can while he clamped the engine to the side of the kitchen sink and started it. She agreed. The 28-year-old man managed to start

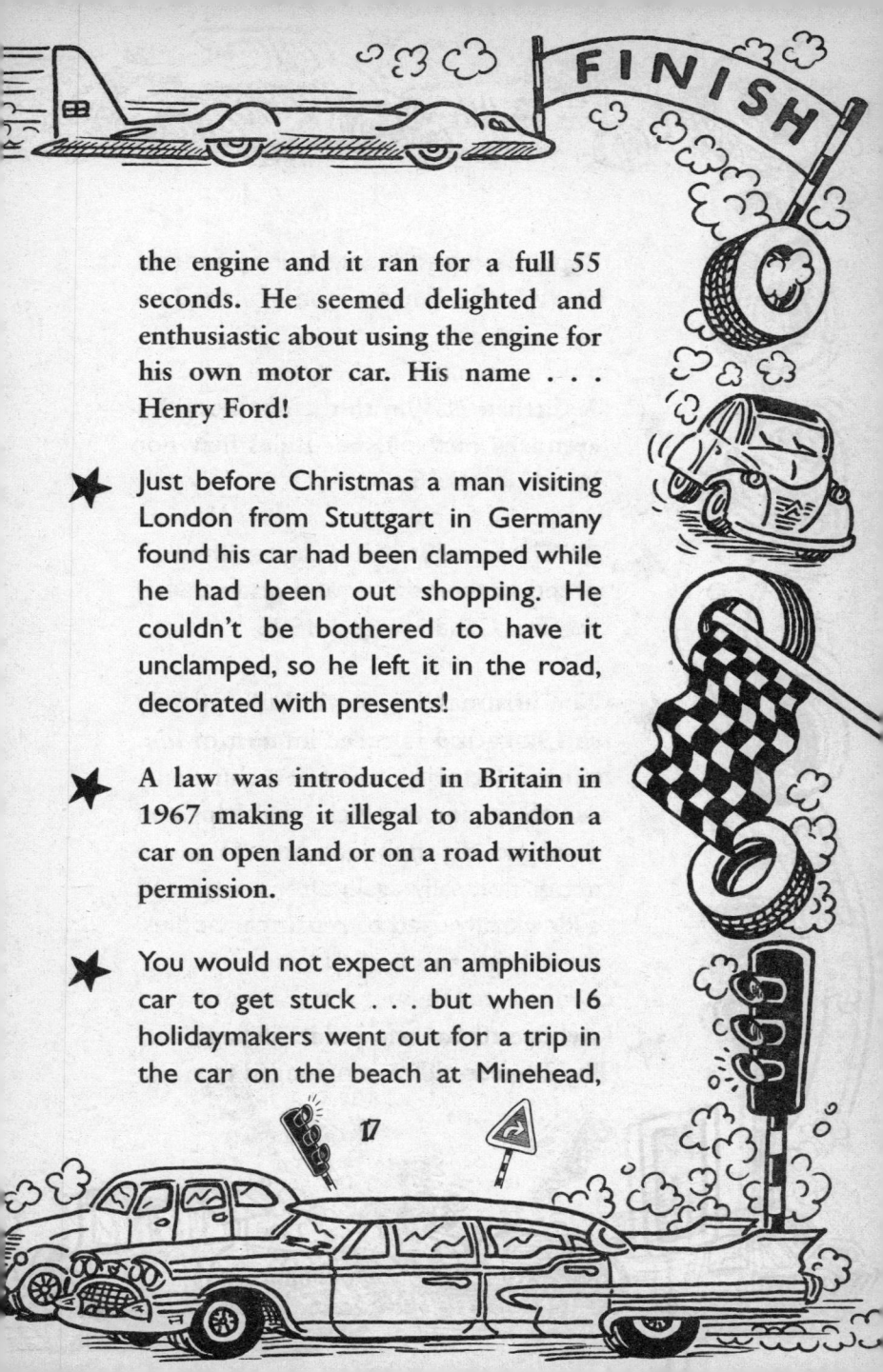

FINISH

the engine and it ran for a full 55 seconds. He seemed delighted and enthusiastic about using the engine for his own motor car. His name . . . Henry Ford!

★ Just before Christmas a man visiting London from Stuttgart in Germany found his car had been clamped while he had been out shopping. He couldn't be bothered to have it unclamped, so he left it in the road, decorated with presents!

★ A law was introduced in Britain in 1967 making it illegal to abandon a car on open land or on a road without permission.

★ You would not expect an amphibious car to get stuck . . . but when 16 holidaymakers went out for a trip in the car on the beach at Minehead,

17

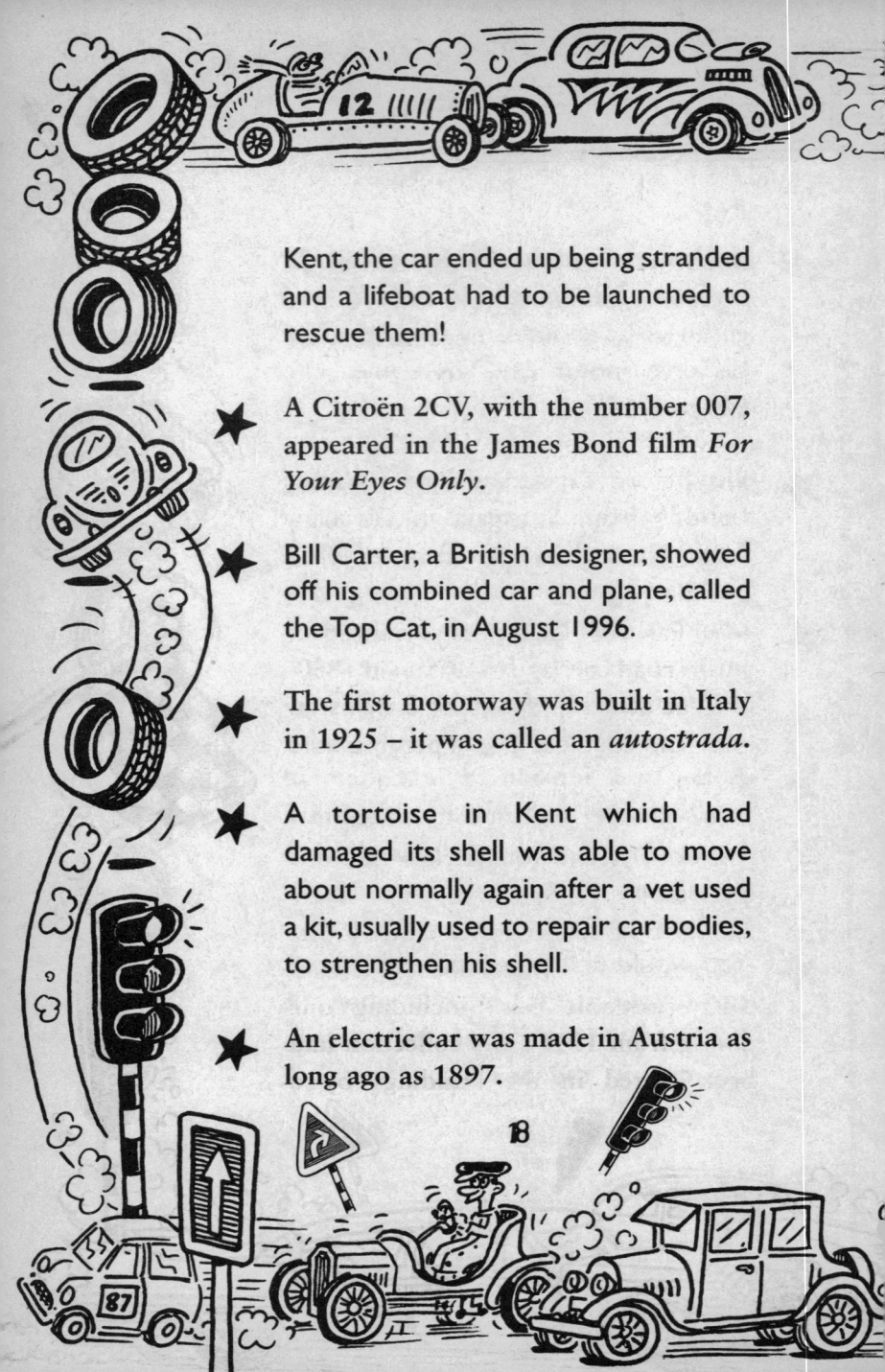

Kent, the car ended up being stranded and a lifeboat had to be launched to rescue them!

★ A Citroën 2CV, with the number 007, appeared in the James Bond film *For Your Eyes Only*.

★ Bill Carter, a British designer, showed off his combined car and plane, called the Top Cat, in August 1996.

★ The first motorway was built in Italy in 1925 – it was called an *autostrada*.

★ A tortoise in Kent which had damaged its shell was able to move about normally again after a vet used a kit, usually used to repair car bodies, to strengthen his shell.

★ An electric car was made in Austria as long ago as 1897.

FINISH

★ Dorothy Pullinger was the first woman in Britain to take charge of a car factory, when she became head of the Galloway cars company in Scotland, in 1921.

★ At the world sports car championship race in 1992, only three of the cars finished.

★ The Earl of Caithness invented a steam road carriage in Britain in 1860. It went at a top speed of 8 miles an hour and cost less than a penny a mile to run.

★ An estate agent, looking about some old stables in Somerset some years ago, got the surprise of his life. Inside the tumble-down buildings he found thirty valuable cars, including one dating from 1915. The collection had been stored in the buildings by a

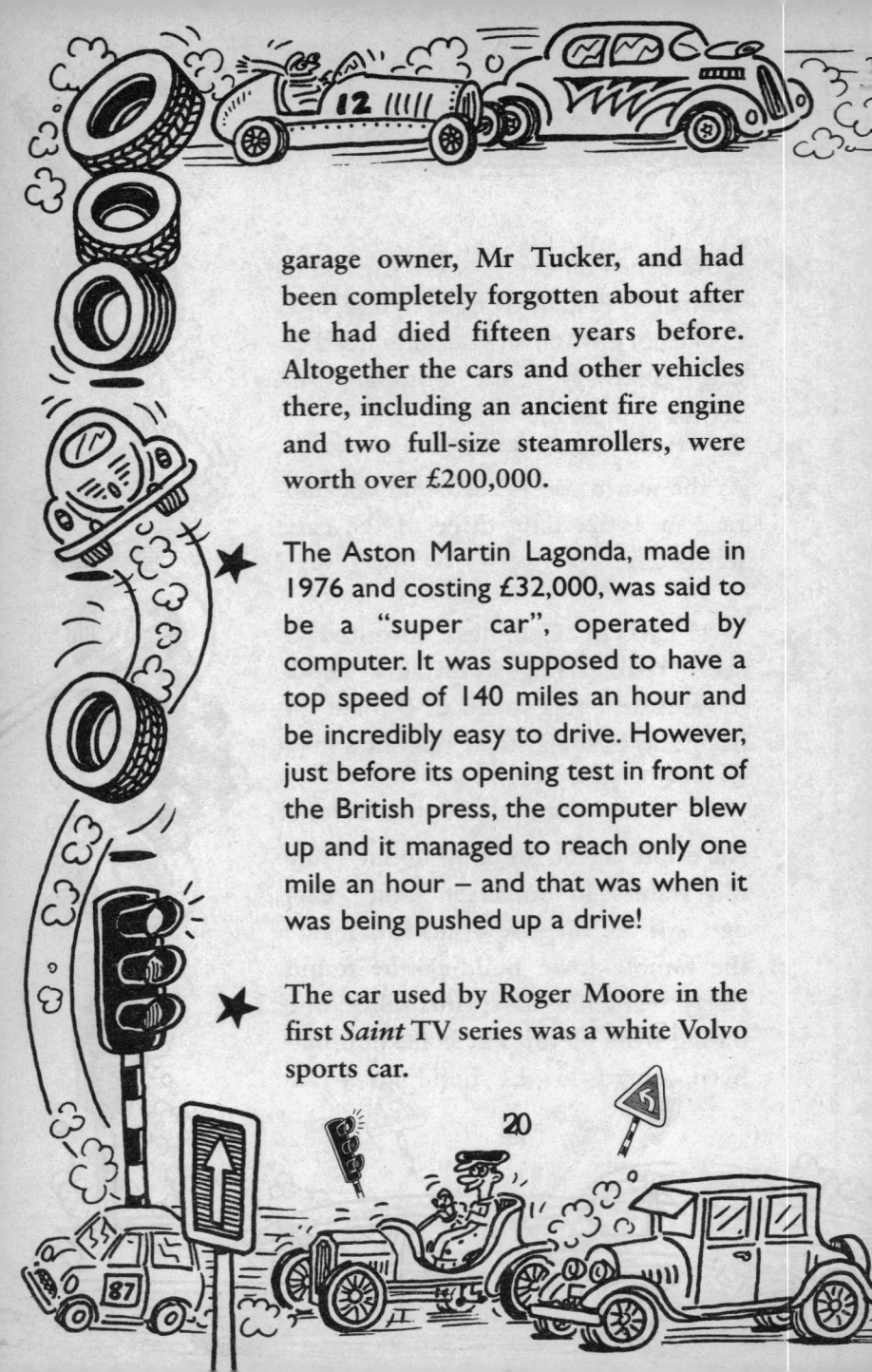

garage owner, Mr Tucker, and had been completely forgotten about after he had died fifteen years before. Altogether the cars and other vehicles there, including an ancient fire engine and two full-size steamrollers, were worth over £200,000.

The Aston Martin Lagonda, made in 1976 and costing £32,000, was said to be a "super car", operated by computer. It was supposed to have a top speed of 140 miles an hour and be incredibly easy to drive. However, just before its opening test in front of the British press, the computer blew up and it managed to reach only one mile an hour — and that was when it was being pushed up a drive!

The car used by Roger Moore in the first *Saint* TV series was a white Volvo sports car.

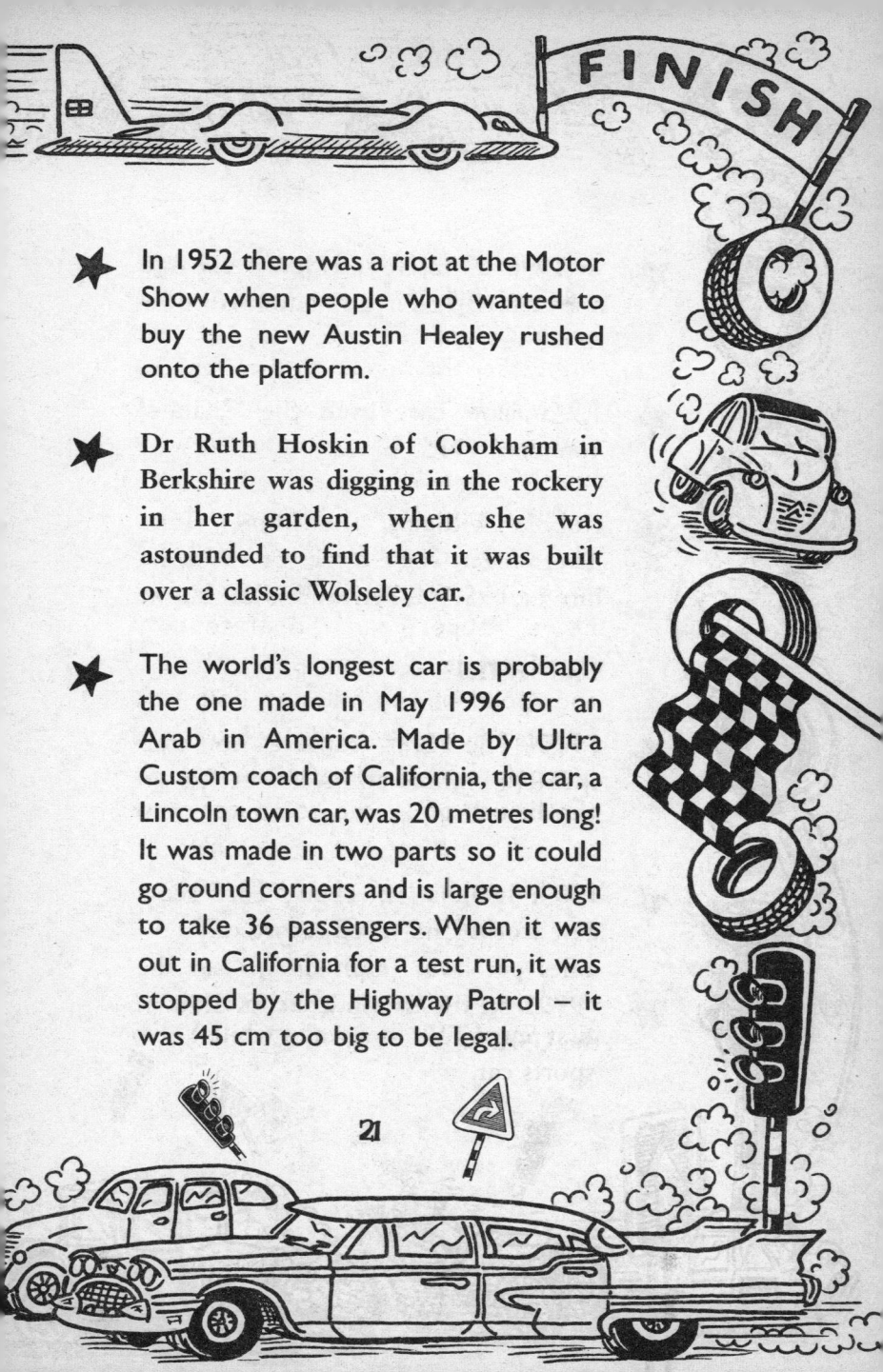

★ In 1952 there was a riot at the Motor Show when people who wanted to buy the new Austin Healey rushed onto the platform.

★ Dr Ruth Hoskin of Cookham in Berkshire was digging in the rockery in her garden, when she was astounded to find that it was built over a classic Wolseley car.

★ The world's longest car is probably the one made in May 1996 for an Arab in America. Made by Ultra Custom coach of California, the car, a Lincoln town car, was 20 metres long! It was made in two parts so it could go round corners and is large enough to take 36 passengers. When it was out in California for a test run, it was stopped by the Highway Patrol — it was 45 cm too big to be legal.

21

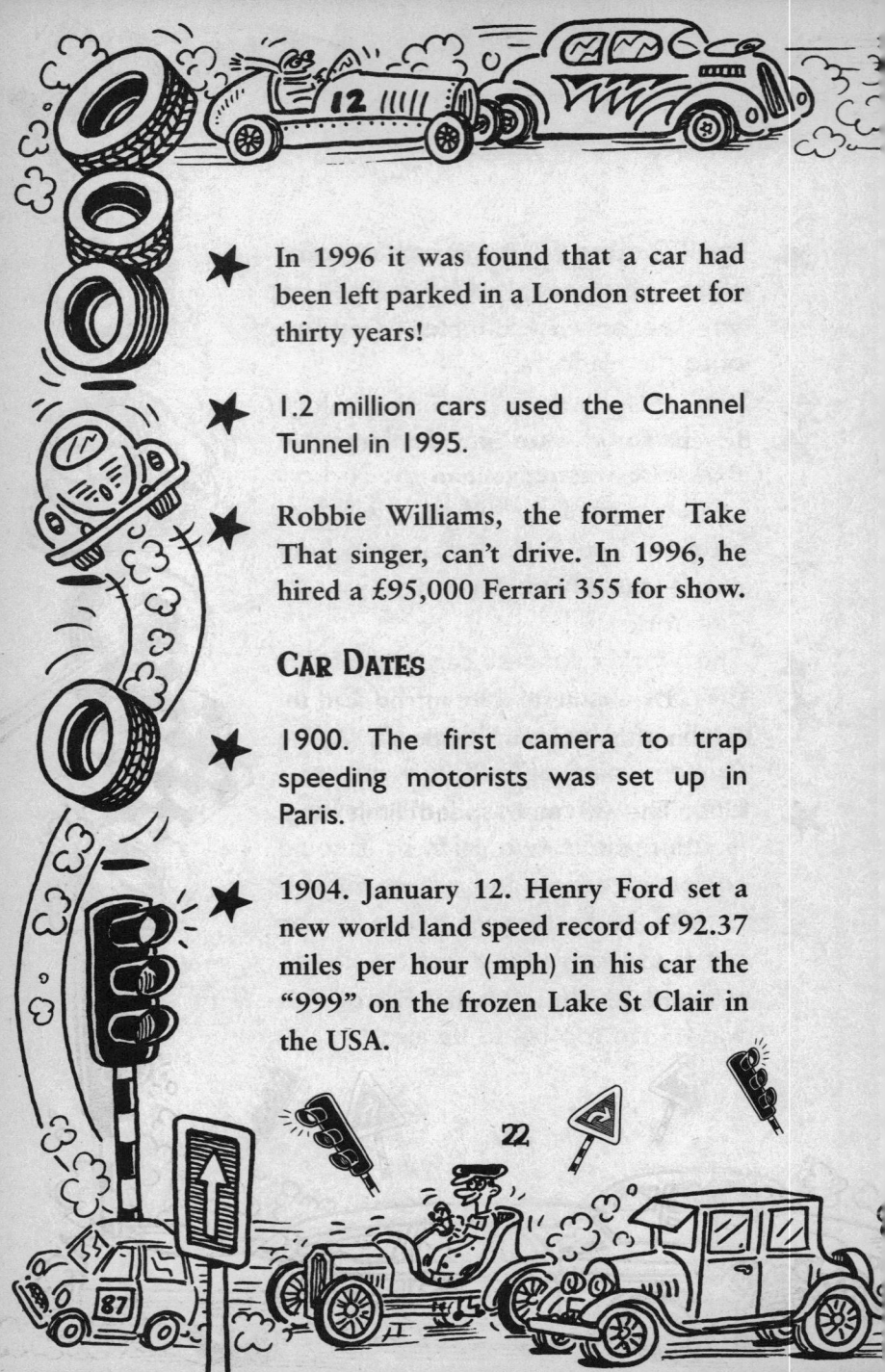

★ In 1996 it was found that a car had been left parked in a London street for thirty years!

★ 1.2 million cars used the Channel Tunnel in 1995.

★ Robbie Williams, the former Take That singer, can't drive. In 1996, he hired a £95,000 Ferrari 355 for show.

CAR DATES

★ 1900. The first camera to trap speeding motorists was set up in Paris.

★ 1904. January 12. Henry Ford set a new world land speed record of 92.37 miles per hour (mph) in his car the "999" on the frozen Lake St Clair in the USA.

22

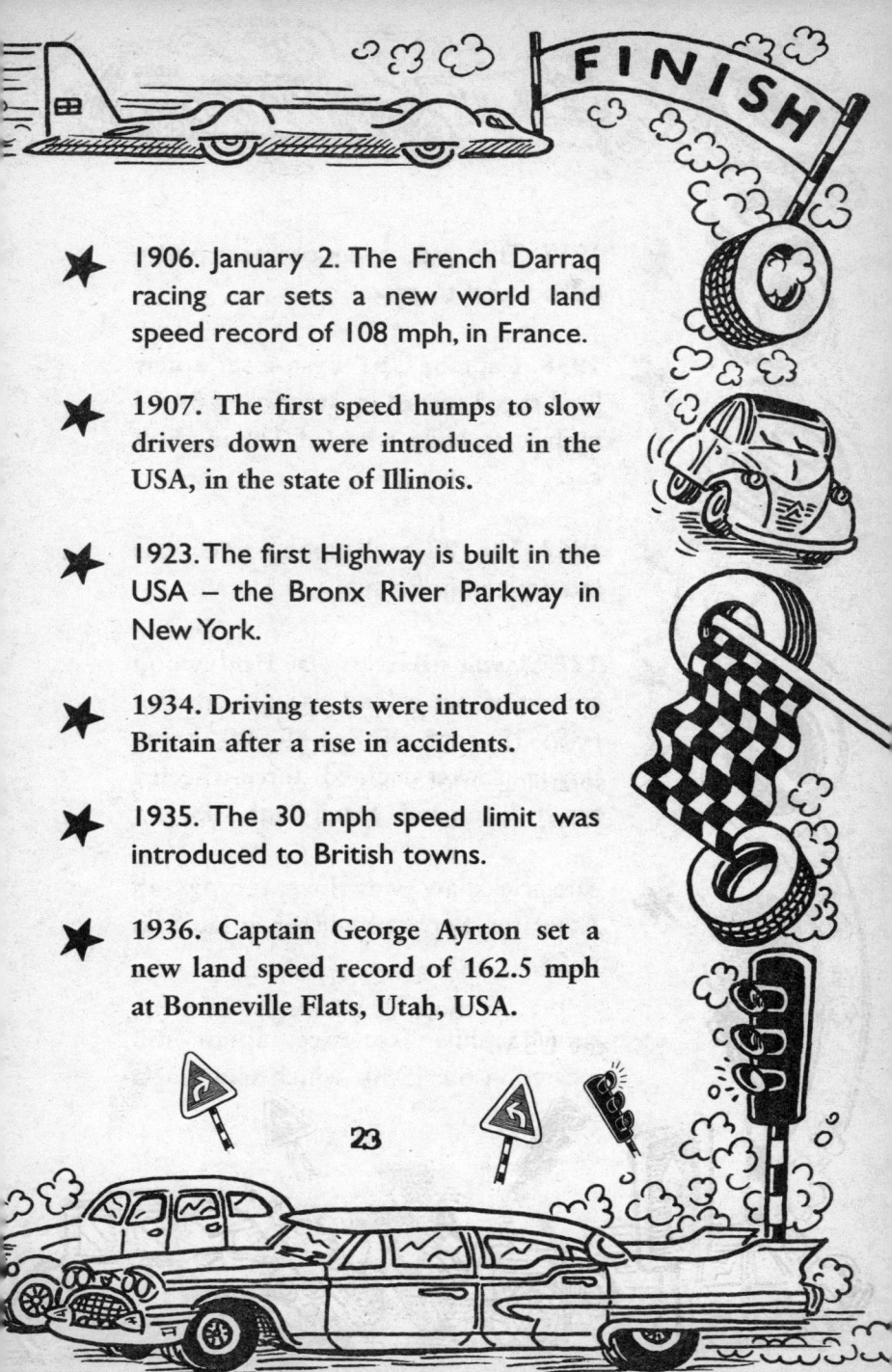

★ 1906. January 2. The French Darraq racing car sets a new world land speed record of 108 mph, in France.

★ 1907. The first speed humps to slow drivers down were introduced in the USA, in the state of Illinois.

★ 1923. The first Highway is built in the USA – the Bronx River Parkway in New York.

★ 1934. Driving tests were introduced to Britain after a rise in accidents.

★ 1935. The 30 mph speed limit was introduced to British towns.

★ 1936. Captain George Ayrton set a new land speed record of 162.5 mph at Bonneville Flats, Utah, USA.

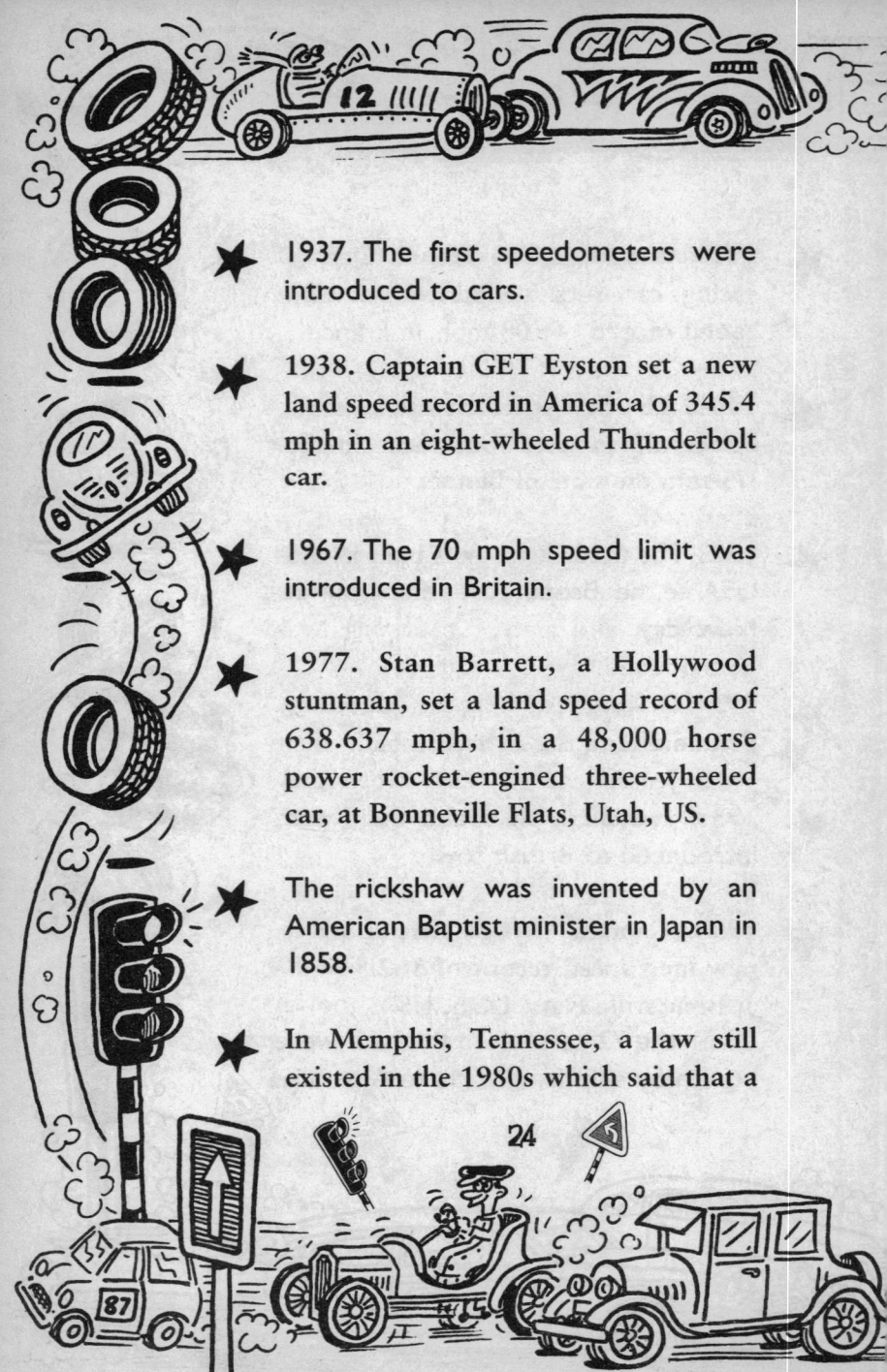

★ 1937. The first speedometers were introduced to cars.

★ 1938. Captain GET Eyston set a new land speed record in America of 345.4 mph in an eight-wheeled Thunderbolt car.

★ 1967. The 70 mph speed limit was introduced in Britain.

★ 1977. Stan Barrett, a Hollywood stuntman, set a land speed record of 638.637 mph, in a 48,000 horse power rocket-engined three-wheeled car, at Bonneville Flats, Utah, US.

★ The rickshaw was invented by an American Baptist minister in Japan in 1858.

★ In Memphis, Tennessee, a law still existed in the 1980s which said that a

24

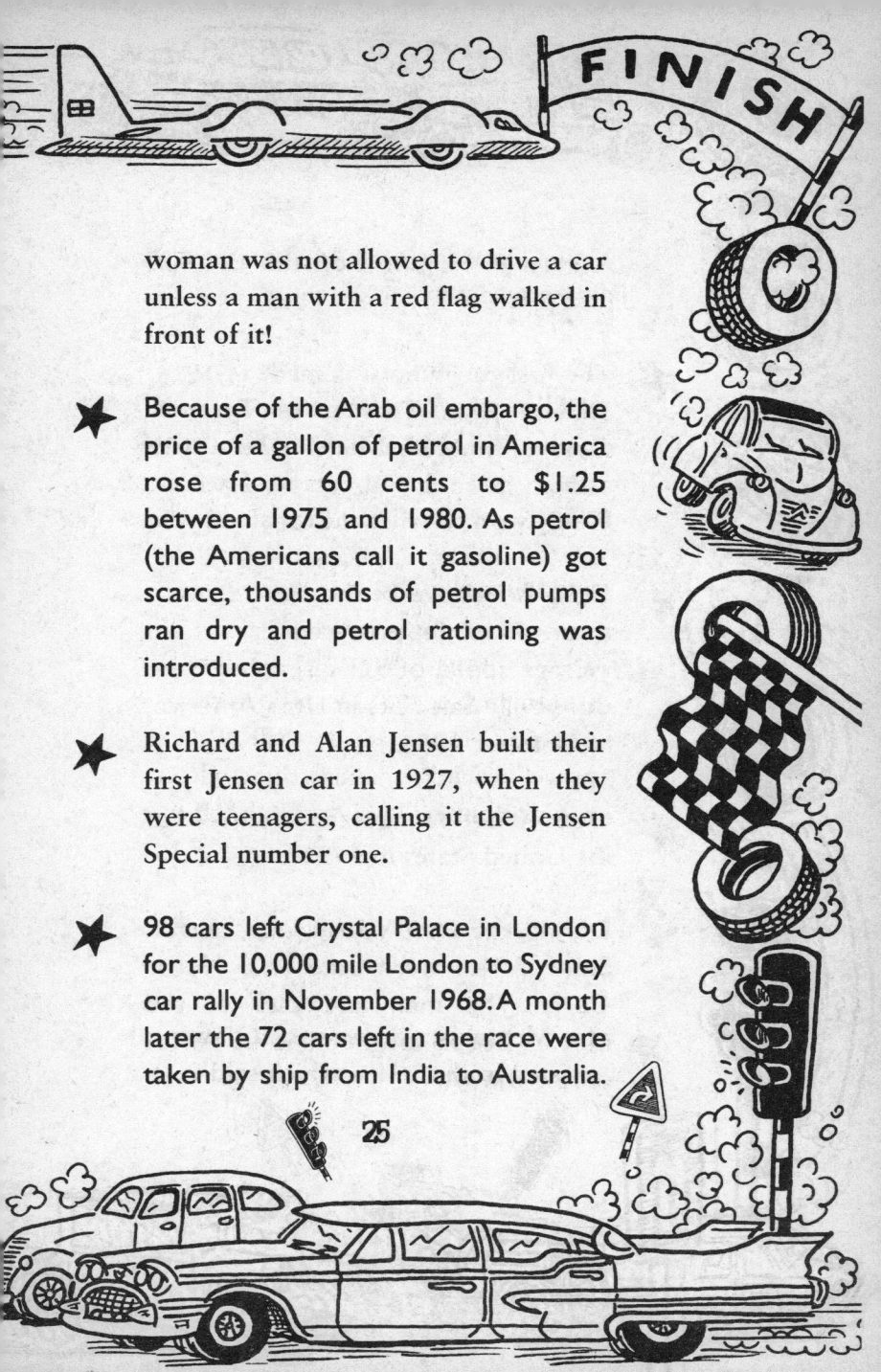

woman was not allowed to drive a car unless a man with a red flag walked in front of it!

★ Because of the Arab oil embargo, the price of a gallon of petrol in America rose from 60 cents to $1.25 between 1975 and 1980. As petrol (the Americans call it gasoline) got scarce, thousands of petrol pumps ran dry and petrol rationing was introduced.

★ Richard and Alan Jensen built their first Jensen car in 1927, when they were teenagers, calling it the Jensen Special number one.

★ 98 cars left Crystal Palace in London for the 10,000 mile London to Sydney car rally in November 1968. A month later the 72 cars left in the race were taken by ship from India to Australia.

25

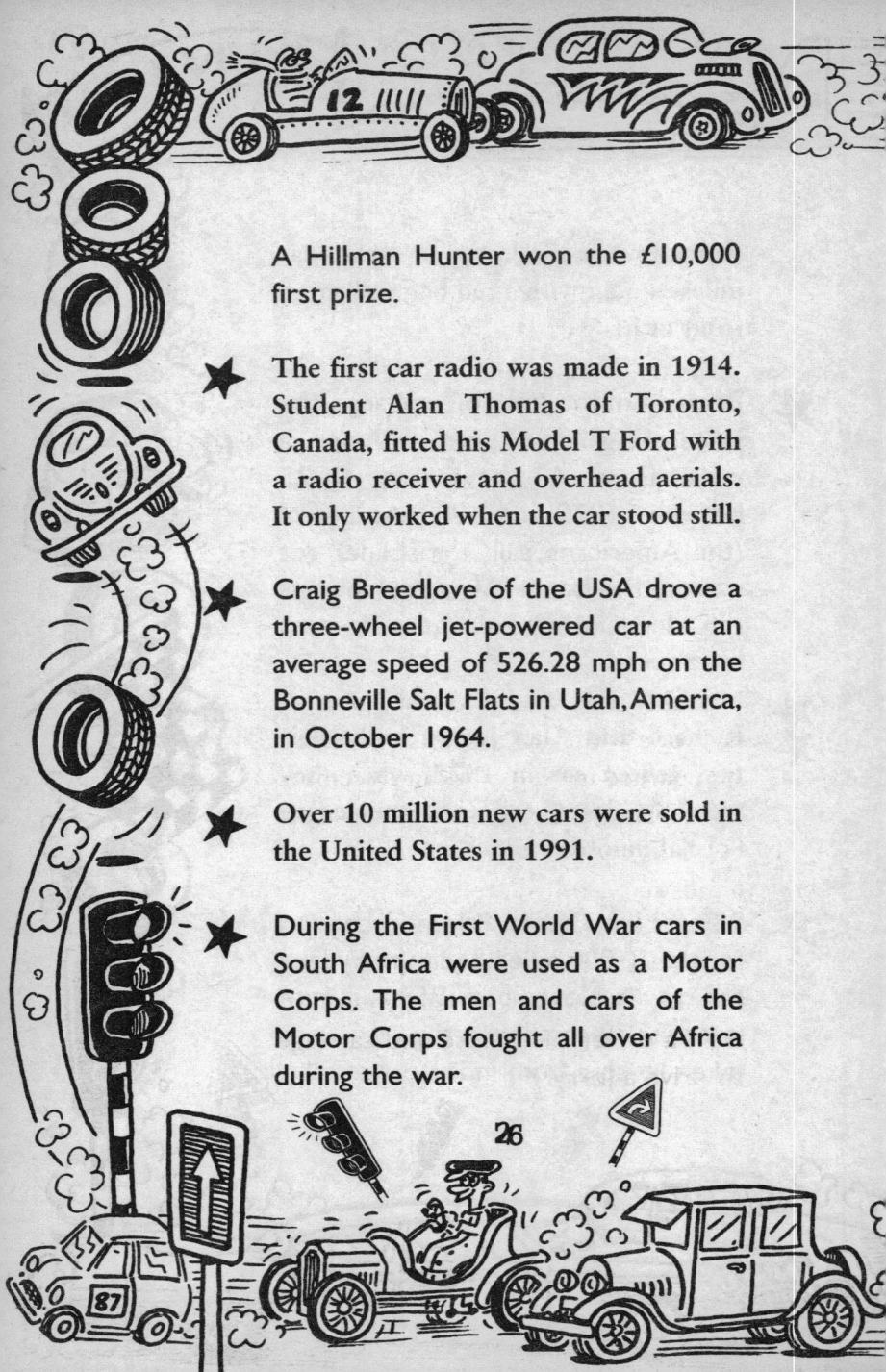

A Hillman Hunter won the £10,000 first prize.

★ The first car radio was made in 1914. Student Alan Thomas of Toronto, Canada, fitted his Model T Ford with a radio receiver and overhead aerials. It only worked when the car stood still.

★ Craig Breedlove of the USA drove a three-wheel jet-powered car at an average speed of 526.28 mph on the Bonneville Salt Flats in Utah, America, in October 1964.

★ Over 10 million new cars were sold in the United States in 1991.

★ During the First World War cars in South Africa were used as a Motor Corps. The men and cars of the Motor Corps fought all over Africa during the war.

26

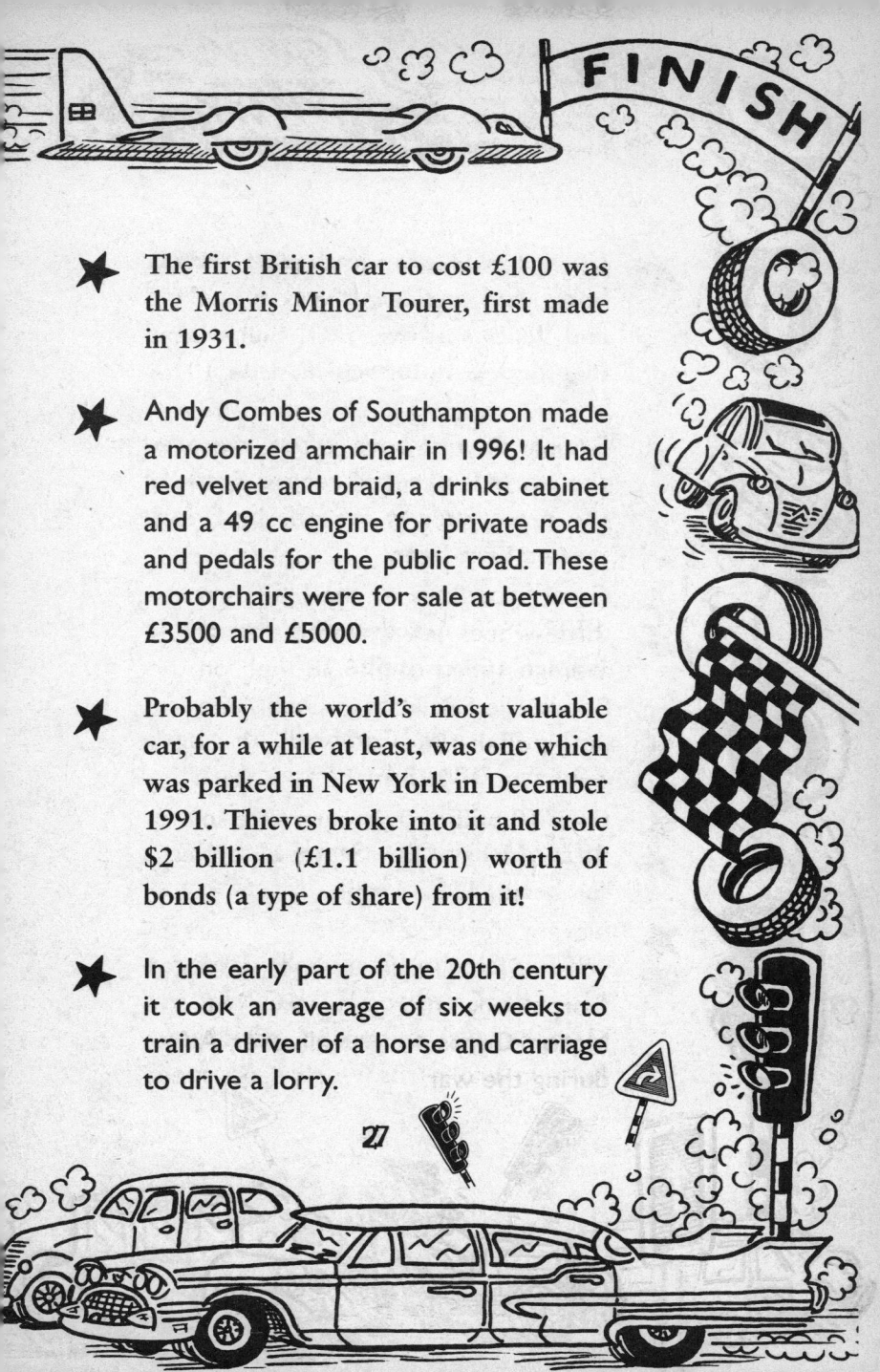

★ The first British car to cost £100 was the Morris Minor Tourer, first made in 1931.

★ Andy Combes of Southampton made a motorized armchair in 1996! It had red velvet and braid, a drinks cabinet and a 49 cc engine for private roads and pedals for the public road. These motorchairs were for sale at between £3500 and £5000.

★ Probably the world's most valuable car, for a while at least, was one which was parked in New York in December 1991. Thieves broke into it and stole $2 billion (£1.1 billion) worth of bonds (a type of share) from it!

★ In the early part of the 20th century it took an average of six weeks to train a driver of a horse and carriage to drive a lorry.

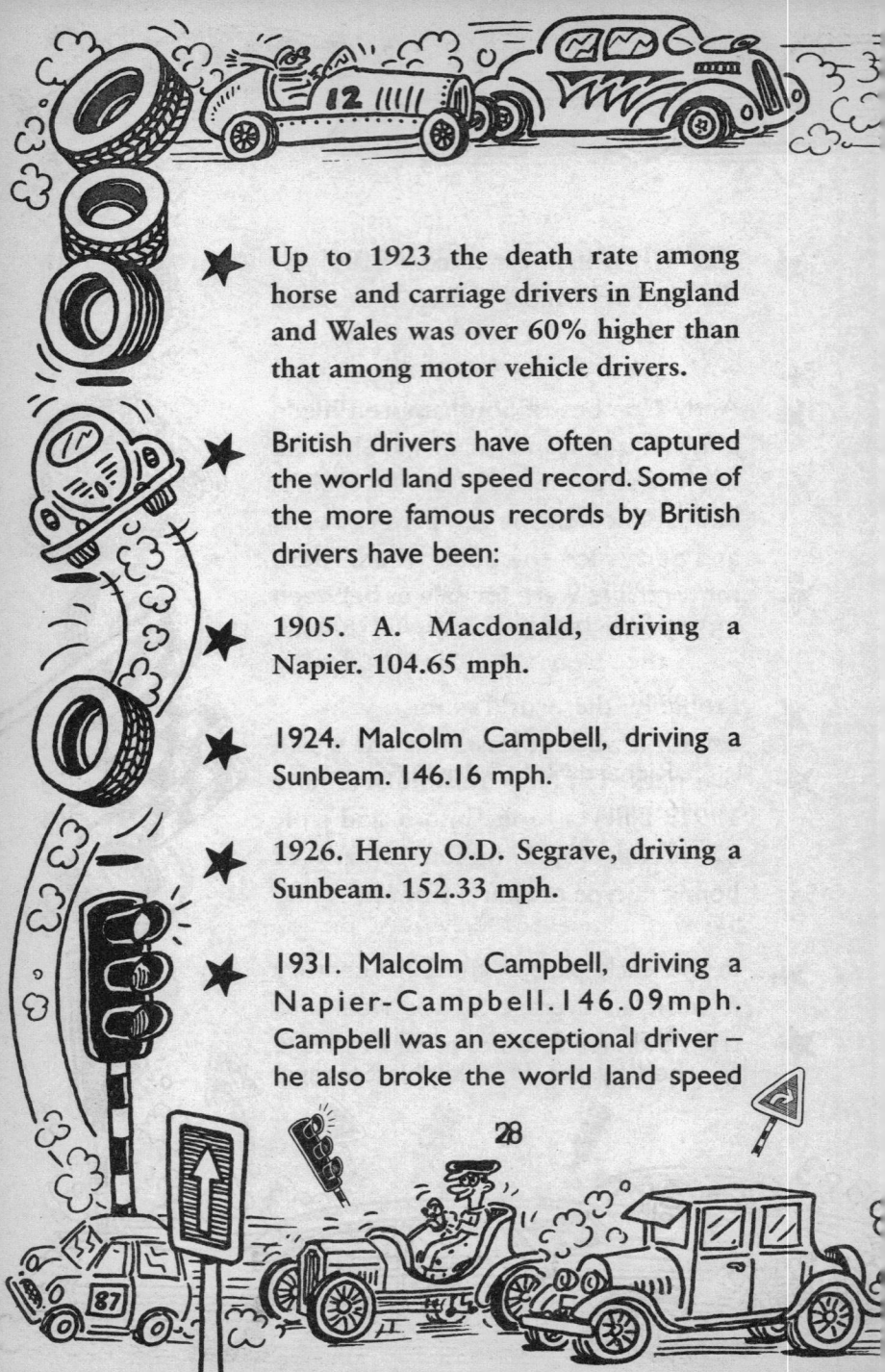

★ Up to 1923 the death rate among horse and carriage drivers in England and Wales was over 60% higher than that among motor vehicle drivers.

★ British drivers have often captured the world land speed record. Some of the more famous records by British drivers have been:

★ 1905. A. Macdonald, driving a Napier. 104.65 mph.

★ 1924. Malcolm Campbell, driving a Sunbeam. 146.16 mph.

★ 1926. Henry O.D. Segrave, driving a Sunbeam. 152.33 mph.

★ 1931. Malcolm Campbell, driving a Napier-Campbell. 146.09 mph. Campbell was an exceptional driver – he also broke the world land speed

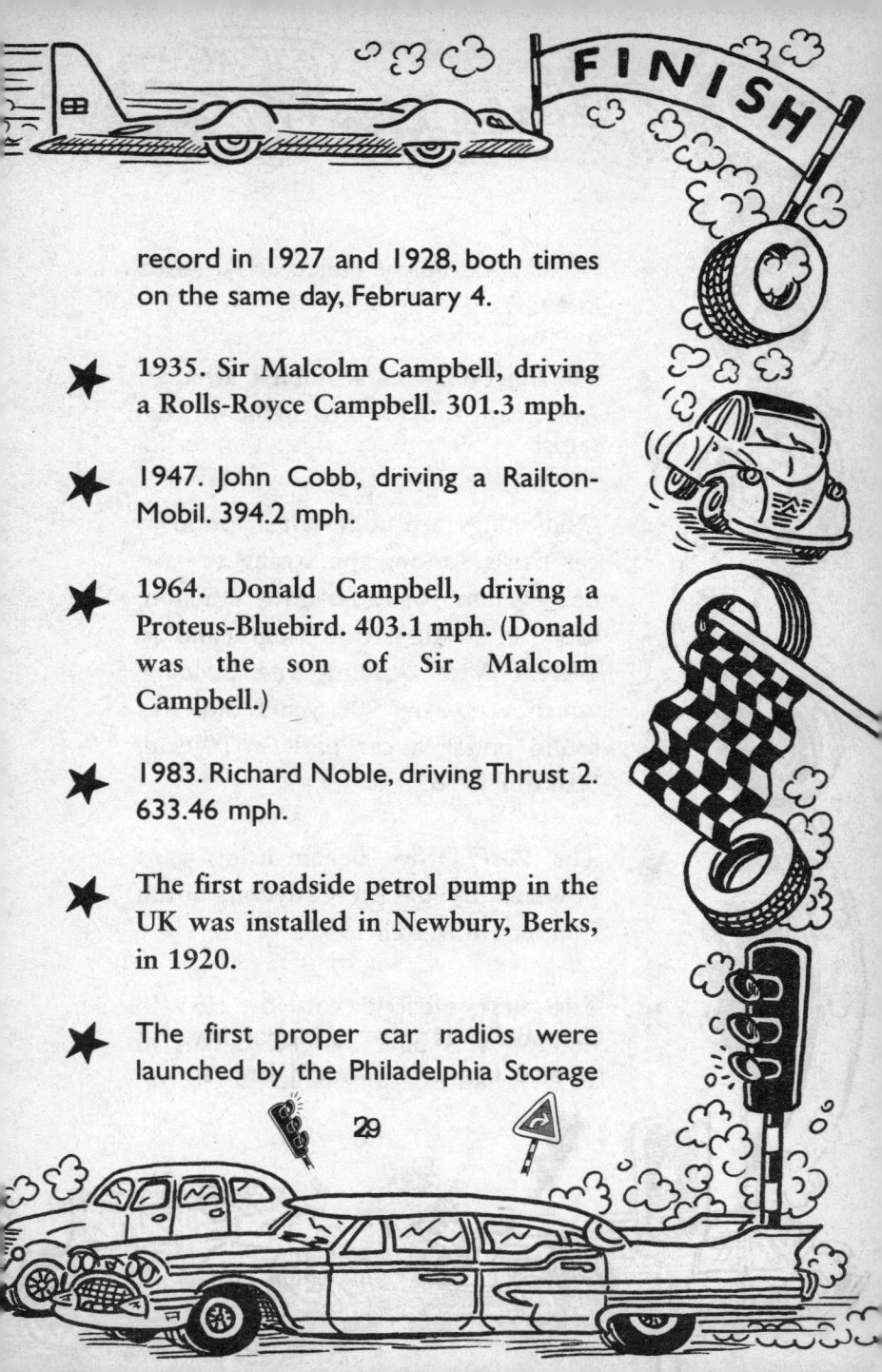

record in 1927 and 1928, both times on the same day, February 4.

★ 1935. Sir Malcolm Campbell, driving a Rolls-Royce Campbell. 301.3 mph.

★ 1947. John Cobb, driving a Railton-Mobil. 394.2 mph.

★ 1964. Donald Campbell, driving a Proteus-Bluebird. 403.1 mph. (Donald was the son of Sir Malcolm Campbell.)

★ 1983. Richard Noble, driving Thrust 2. 633.46 mph.

★ The first roadside petrol pump in the UK was installed in Newbury, Berks, in 1920.

★ The first proper car radios were launched by the Philadelphia Storage

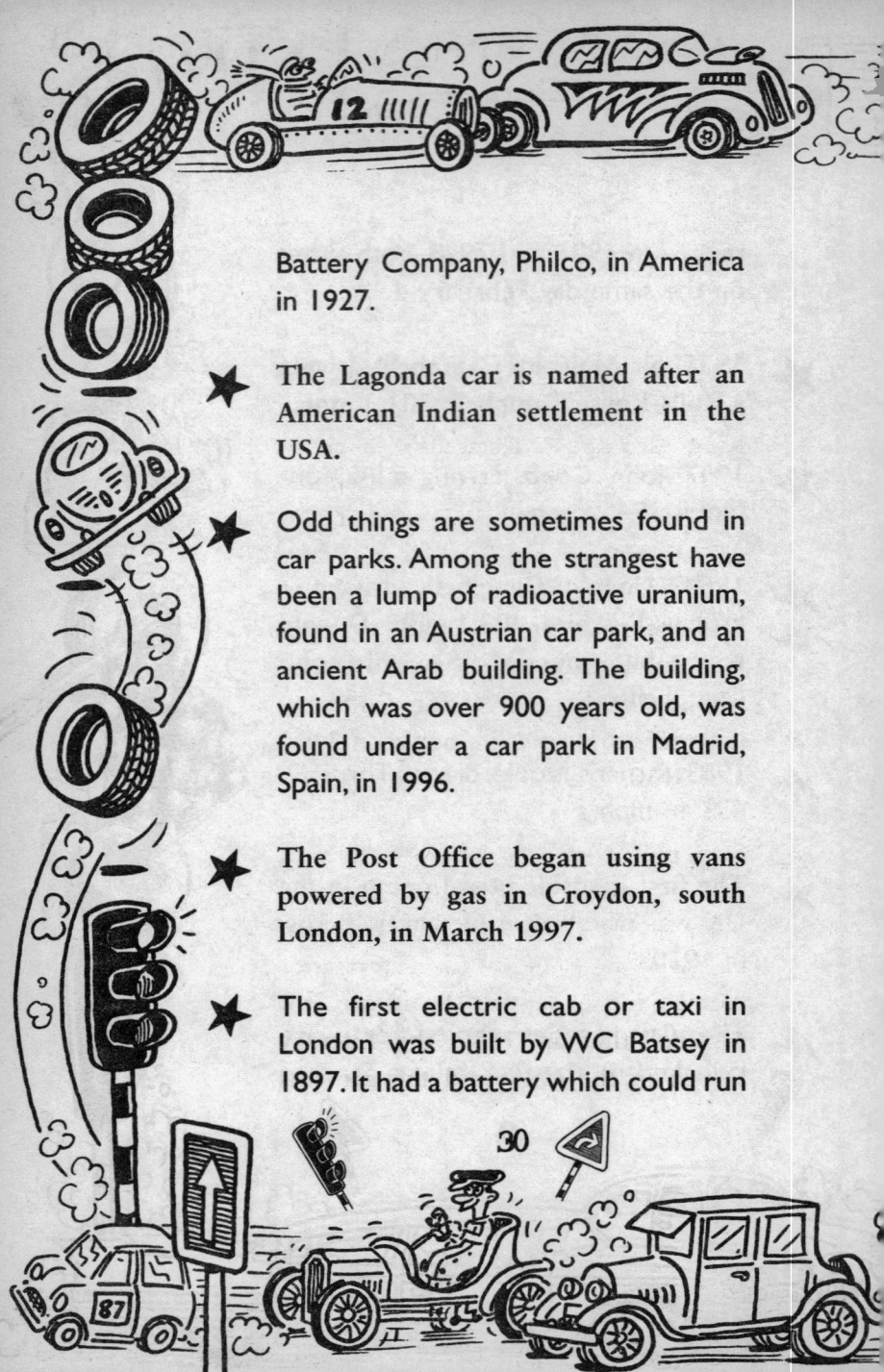

Battery Company, Philco, in America in 1927.

★ The Lagonda car is named after an American Indian settlement in the USA.

★ Odd things are sometimes found in car parks. Among the strangest have been a lump of radioactive uranium, found in an Austrian car park, and an ancient Arab building. The building, which was over 900 years old, was found under a car park in Madrid, Spain, in 1996.

★ The Post Office began using vans powered by gas in Croydon, south London, in March 1997.

★ The first electric cab or taxi in London was built by WC Batsey in 1897. It had a battery which could run

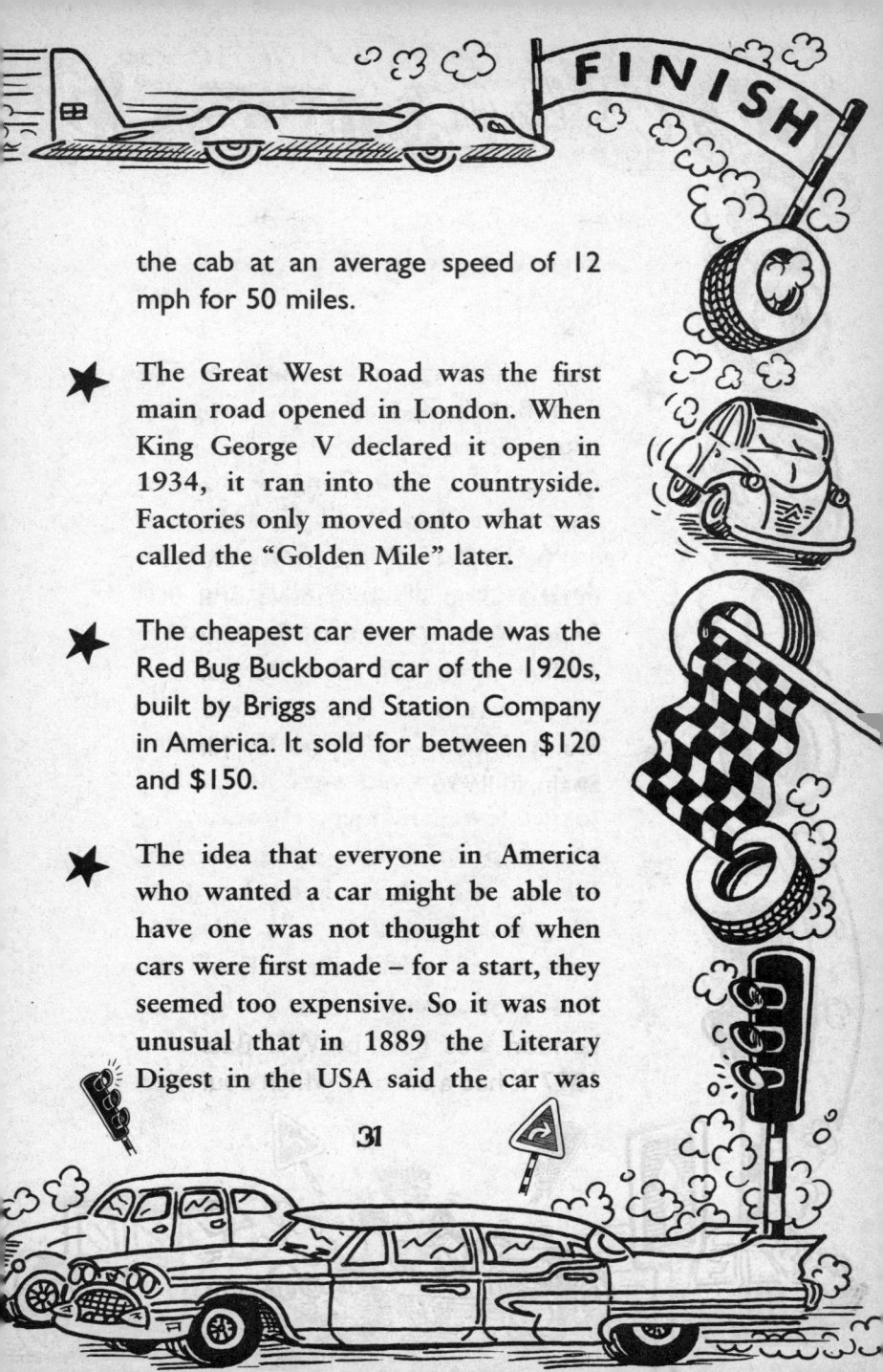

the cab at an average speed of 12 mph for 50 miles.

★ The Great West Road was the first main road opened in London. When King George V declared it open in 1934, it ran into the countryside. Factories only moved onto what was called the "Golden Mile" later.

★ The cheapest car ever made was the Red Bug Buckboard car of the 1920s, built by Briggs and Station Company in America. It sold for between $120 and $150.

★ The idea that everyone in America who wanted a car might be able to have one was not thought of when cars were first made – for a start, they seemed too expensive. So it was not unusual that in 1889 the Literary Digest in the USA said the car was

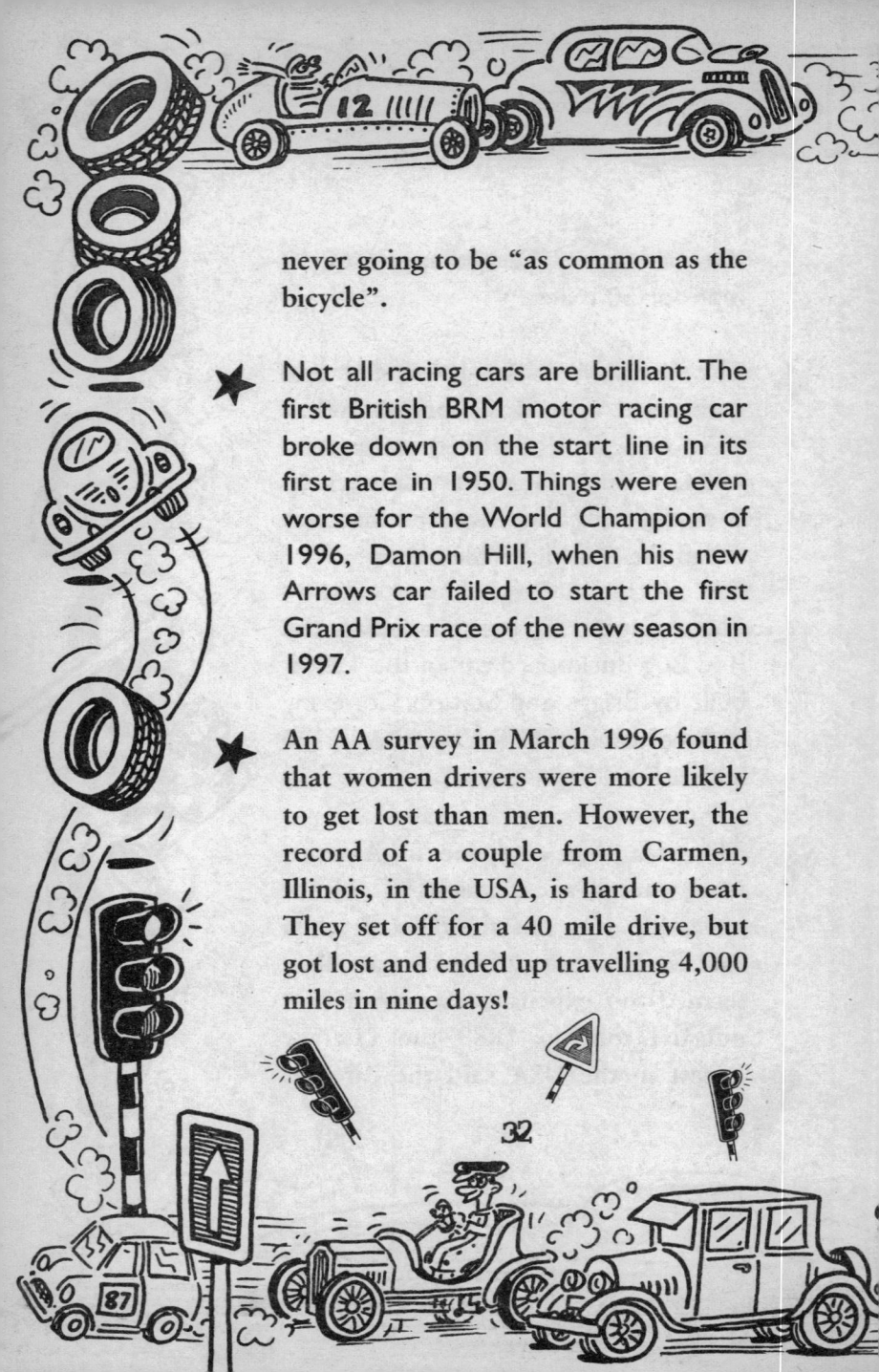

never going to be "as common as the bicycle".

★ Not all racing cars are brilliant. The first British BRM motor racing car broke down on the start line in its first race in 1950. Things were even worse for the World Champion of 1996, Damon Hill, when his new Arrows car failed to start the first Grand Prix race of the new season in 1997.

★ An AA survey in March 1996 found that women drivers were more likely to get lost than men. However, the record of a couple from Carmen, Illinois, in the USA, is hard to beat. They set off for a 40 mile drive, but got lost and ended up travelling 4,000 miles in nine days!

32

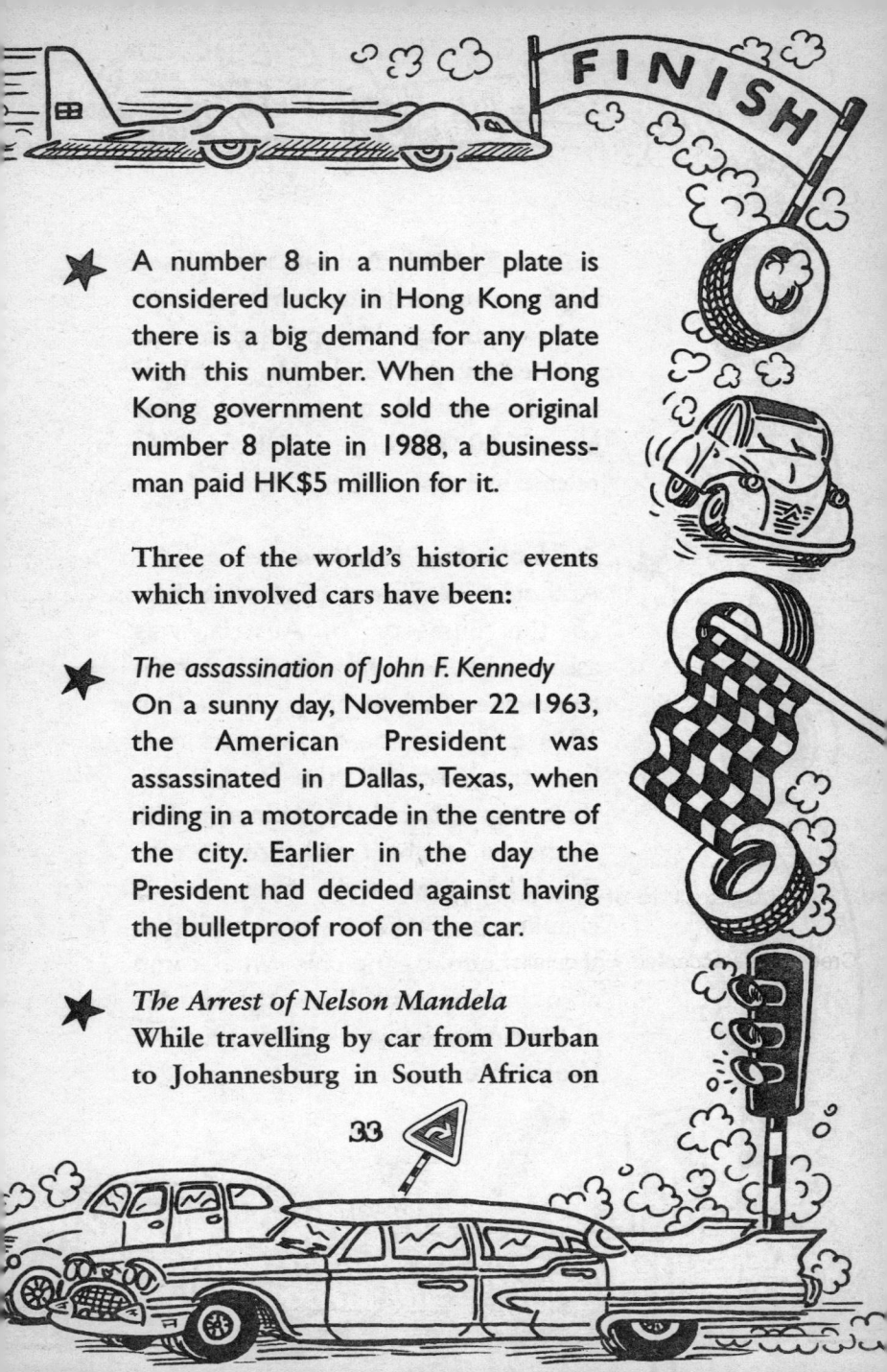

★ A number 8 in a number plate is considered lucky in Hong Kong and there is a big demand for any plate with this number. When the Hong Kong government sold the original number 8 plate in 1988, a businessman paid HK$5 million for it.

Three of the world's historic events which involved cars have been:

★ *The assassination of John F. Kennedy*
On a sunny day, November 22 1963, the American President was assassinated in Dallas, Texas, when riding in a motorcade in the centre of the city. Earlier in the day the President had decided against having the bulletproof roof on the car.

★ *The Arrest of Nelson Mandela*
While travelling by car from Durban to Johannesburg in South Africa on

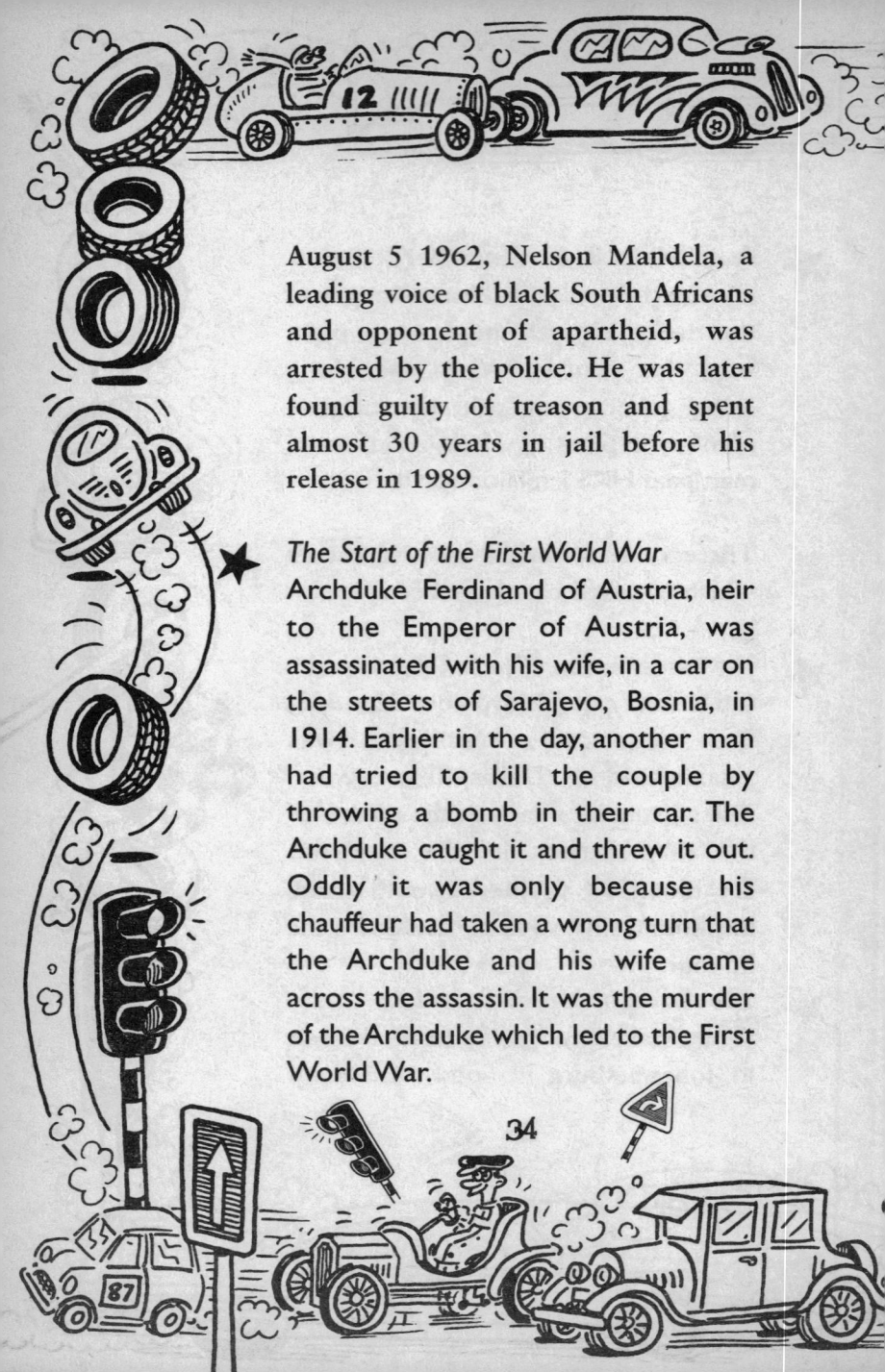

August 5 1962, Nelson Mandela, a leading voice of black South Africans and opponent of apartheid, was arrested by the police. He was later found guilty of treason and spent almost 30 years in jail before his release in 1989.

The Start of the First World War

Archduke Ferdinand of Austria, heir to the Emperor of Austria, was assassinated with his wife, in a car on the streets of Sarajevo, Bosnia, in 1914. Earlier in the day, another man had tried to kill the couple by throwing a bomb in their car. The Archduke caught it and threw it out. Oddly it was only because his chauffeur had taken a wrong turn that the Archduke and his wife came across the assassin. It was the murder of the Archduke which led to the First World War.

34

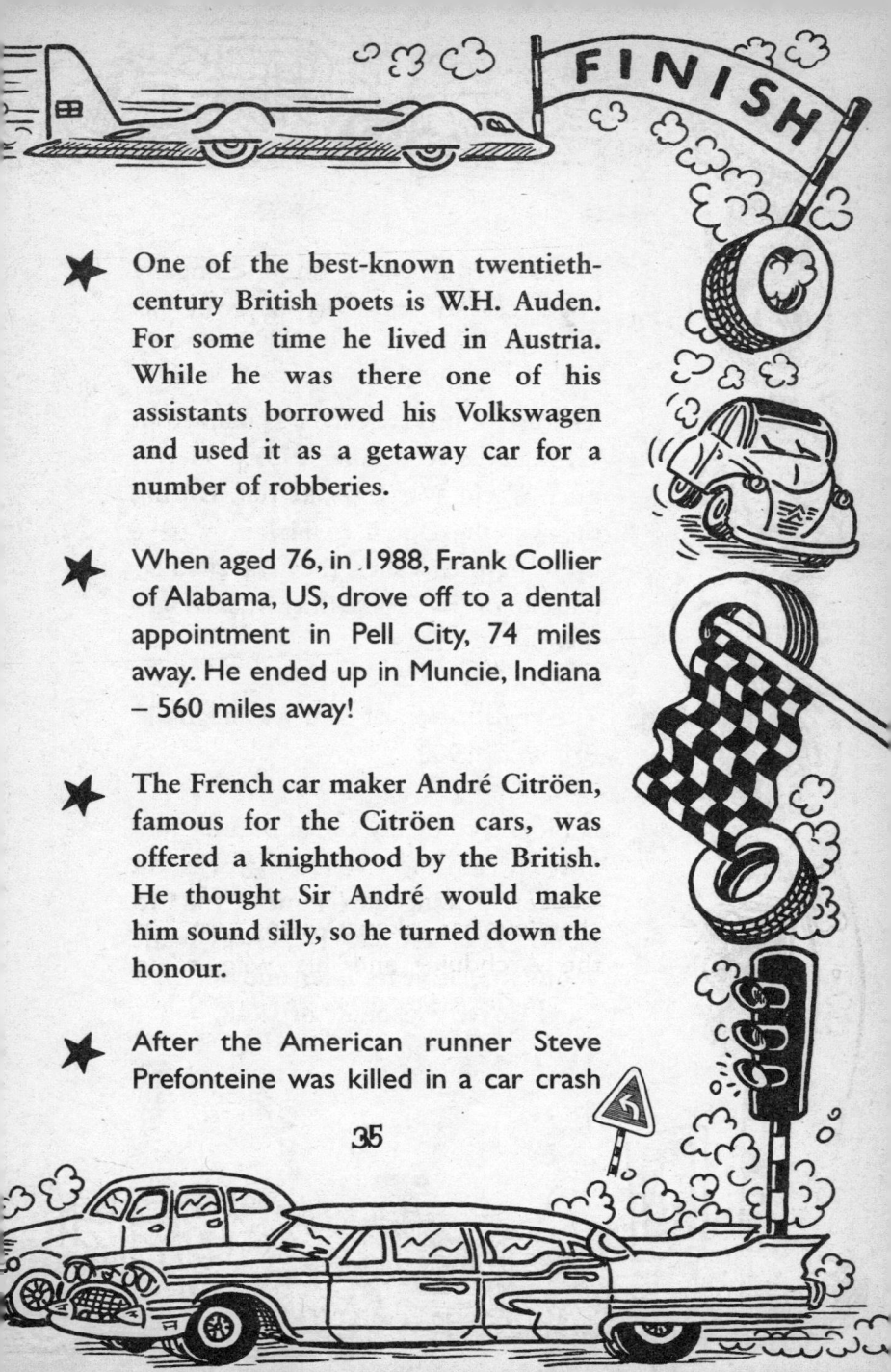

★ One of the best-known twentieth-century British poets is W.H. Auden. For some time he lived in Austria. While he was there one of his assistants borrowed his Volkswagen and used it as a getaway car for a number of robberies.

★ When aged 76, in 1988, Frank Collier of Alabama, US, drove off to a dental appointment in Pell City, 74 miles away. He ended up in Muncie, Indiana — 560 miles away!

★ The French car maker André Citröen, famous for the Citröen cars, was offered a knighthood by the British. He thought Sir André would make him sound silly, so he turned down the honour.

★ After the American runner Steve Prefonteine was killed in a car crash

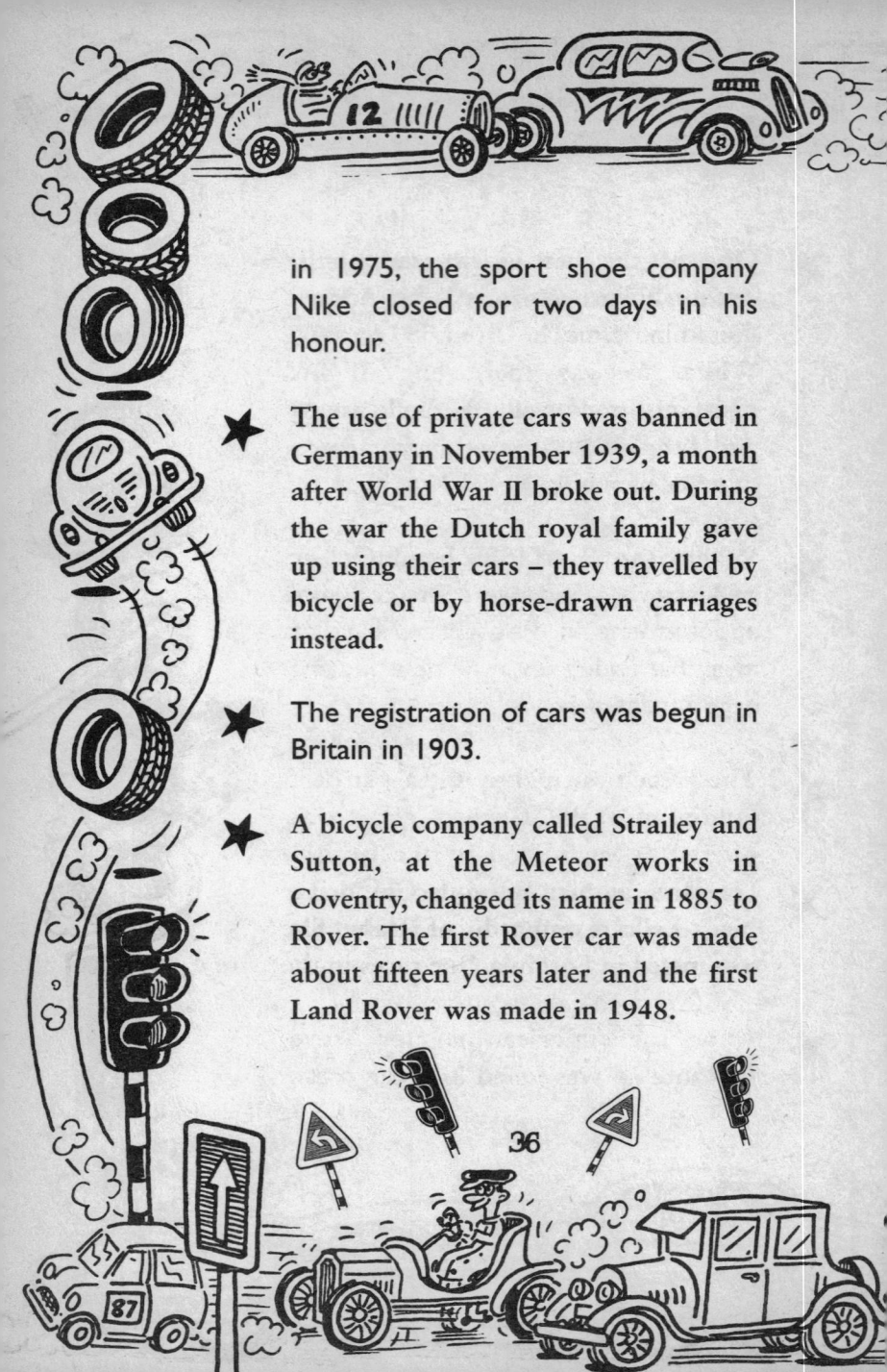

in 1975, the sport shoe company Nike closed for two days in his honour.

★ The use of private cars was banned in Germany in November 1939, a month after World War II broke out. During the war the Dutch royal family gave up using their cars – they travelled by bicycle or by horse-drawn carriages instead.

★ The registration of cars was begun in Britain in 1903.

★ A bicycle company called Strailey and Sutton, at the Meteor works in Coventry, changed its name in 1885 to Rover. The first Rover car was made about fifteen years later and the first Land Rover was made in 1948.

The first car to be pressed out of steel sheets was made by Edward Dudd in the USA.

During the German Grand Prix of 1994, driver Mika Hakkinen caused a big problem. While turning into the first corner he hit another car, which careered across the track, causing a pile-up of 11 out of the 26 cars in the race! They were only 200 metres from the start.

A 1962 Ferrari 250GTO, bought for £5000 in 1971, was sold for £10 million in 1989!

The first woman Formula One driver was Lella Lombardi of Italy. She competed in Formula One races in the 1960s.

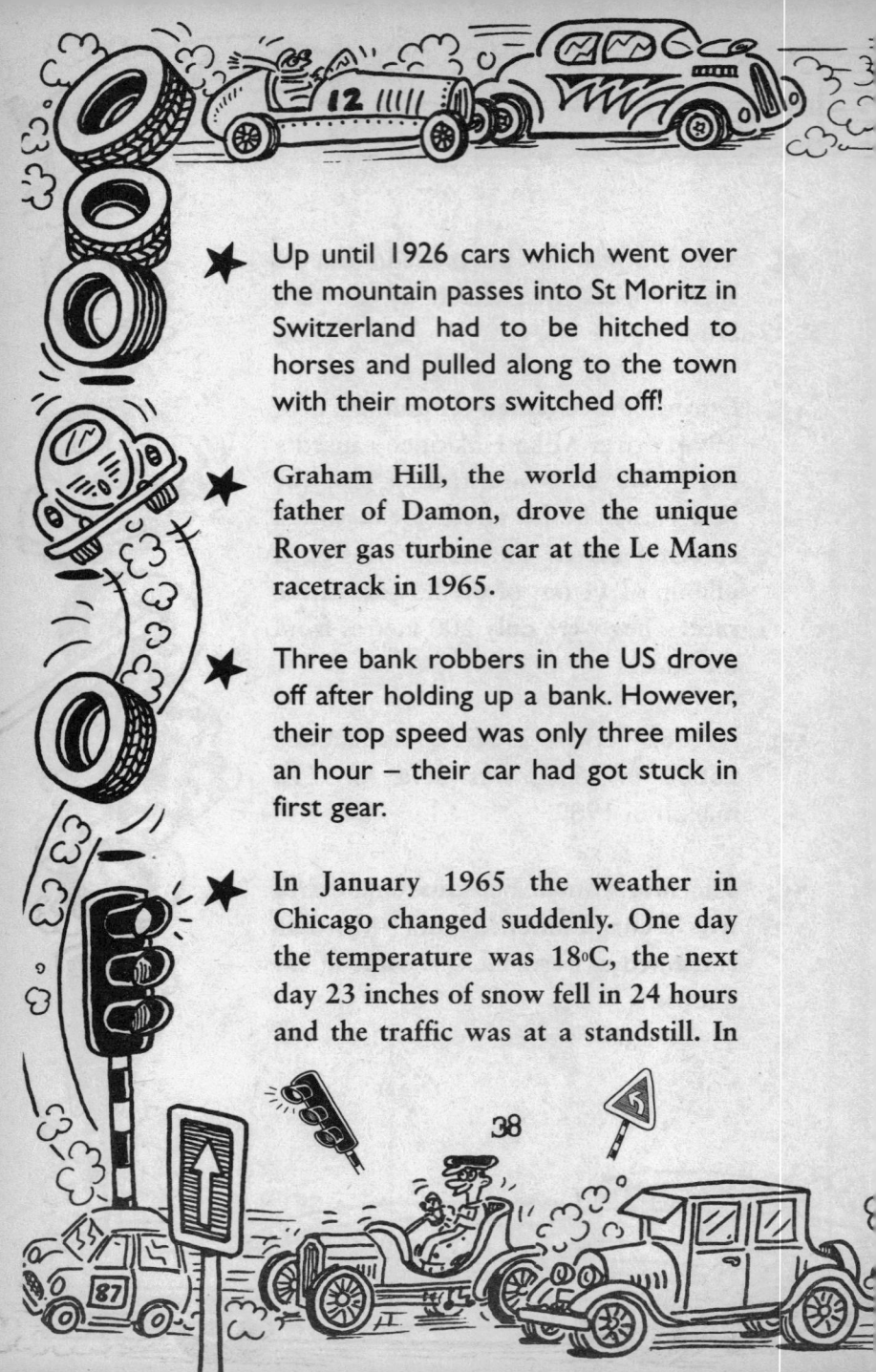

Up until 1926 cars which went over the mountain passes into St Moritz in Switzerland had to be hitched to horses and pulled along to the town with their motors switched off!

Graham Hill, the world champion father of Damon, drove the unique Rover gas turbine car at the Le Mans racetrack in 1965.

Three bank robbers in the US drove off after holding up a bank. However, their top speed was only three miles an hour – their car had got stuck in first gear.

In January 1965 the weather in Chicago changed suddenly. One day the temperature was 18°C, the next day 23 inches of snow fell in 24 hours and the traffic was at a standstill. In

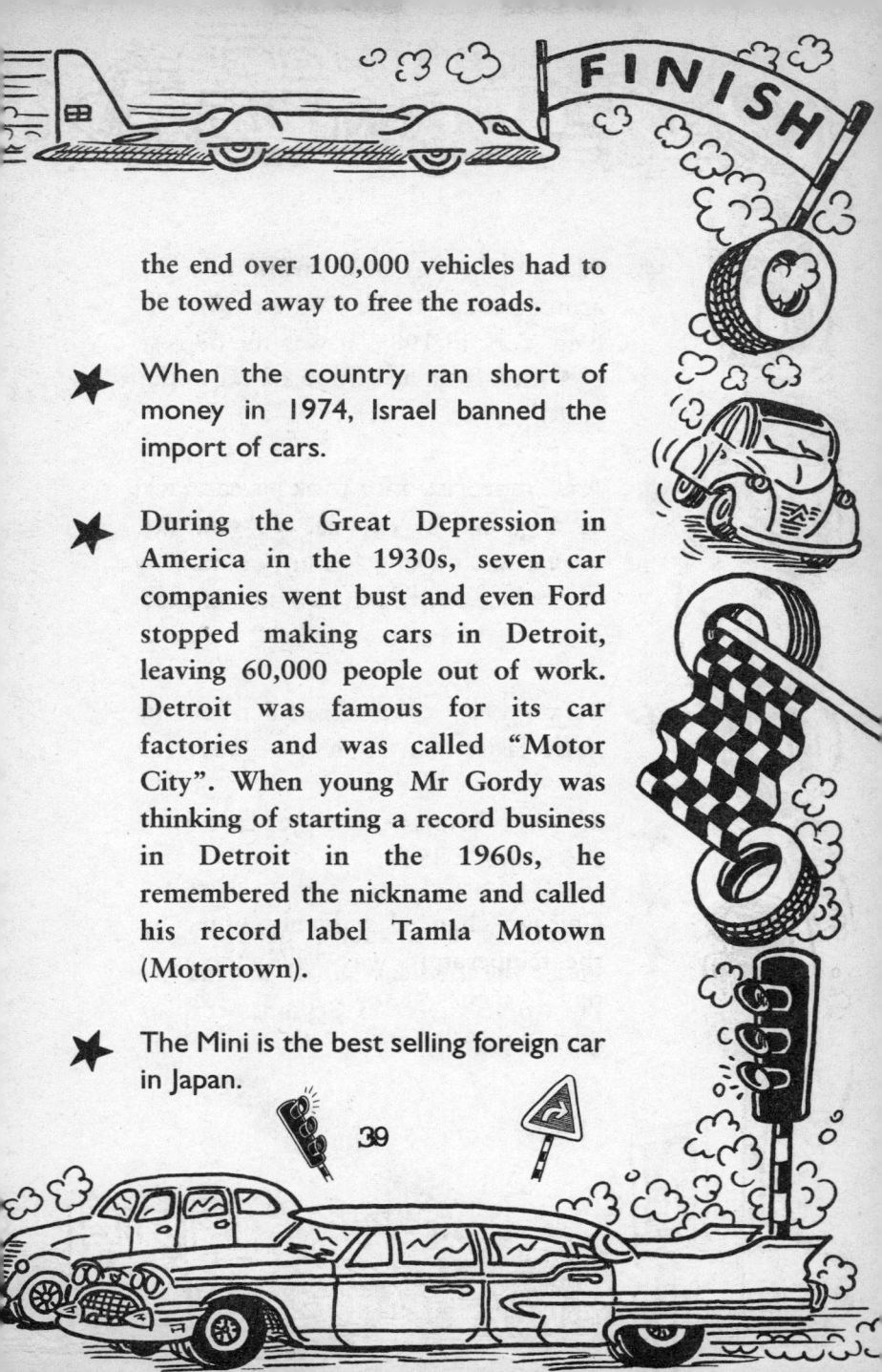

the end over 100,000 vehicles had to be towed away to free the roads.

★ When the country ran short of money in 1974, Israel banned the import of cars.

★ During the Great Depression in America in the 1930s, seven car companies went bust and even Ford stopped making cars in Detroit, leaving 60,000 people out of work. Detroit was famous for its car factories and was called "Motor City". When young Mr Gordy was thinking of starting a record business in Detroit in the 1960s, he remembered the nickname and called his record label Tamla Motown (Motortown).

★ The Mini is the best selling foreign car in Japan.

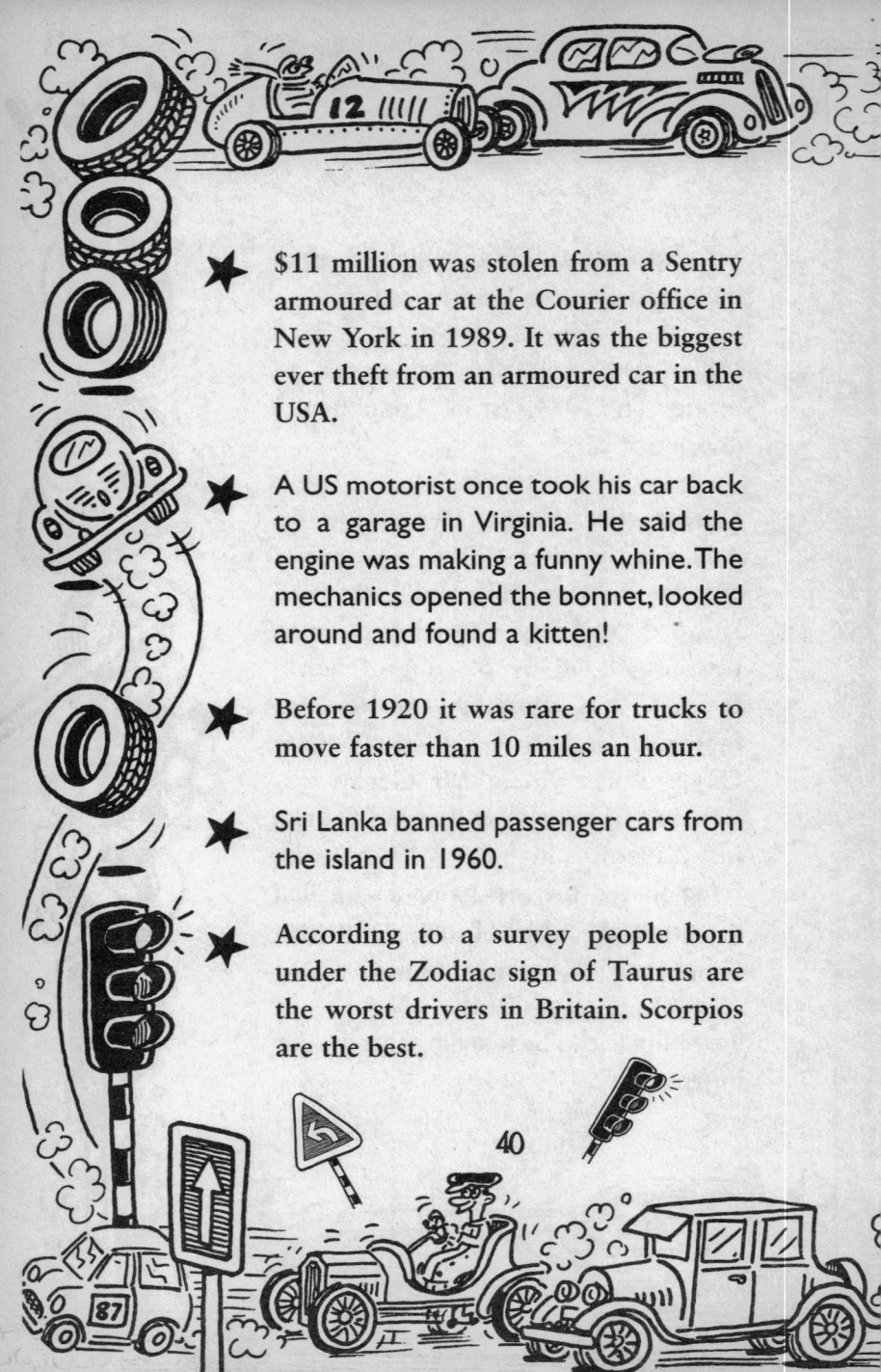

★ $11 million was stolen from a Sentry armoured car at the Courier office in New York in 1989. It was the biggest ever theft from an armoured car in the USA.

★ A US motorist once took his car back to a garage in Virginia. He said the engine was making a funny whine. The mechanics opened the bonnet, looked around and found a kitten!

★ Before 1920 it was rare for trucks to move faster than 10 miles an hour.

★ Sri Lanka banned passenger cars from the island in 1960.

★ According to a survey people born under the Zodiac sign of Taurus are the worst drivers in Britain. Scorpios are the best.

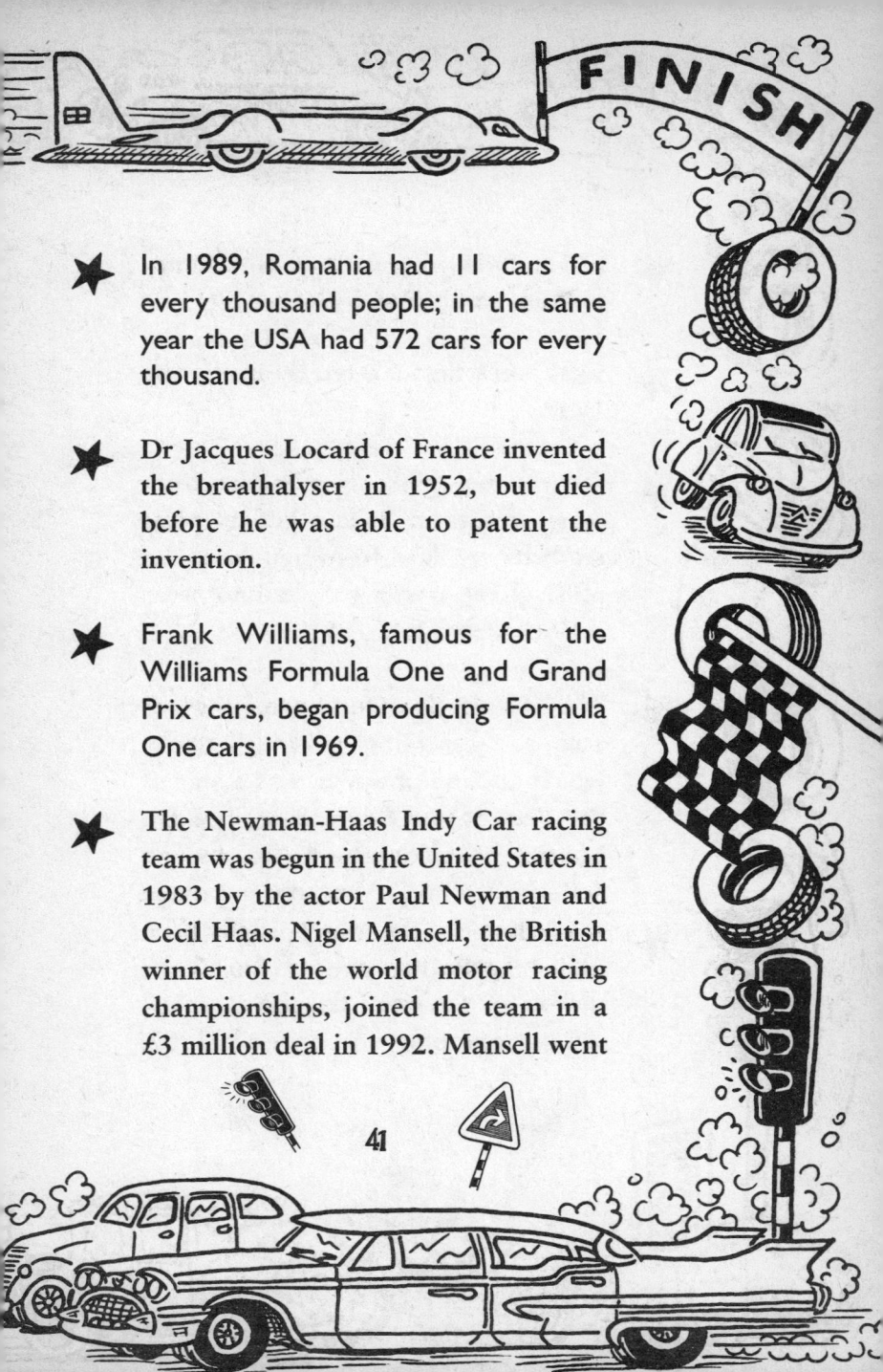

★ In 1989, Romania had 11 cars for every thousand people; in the same year the USA had 572 cars for every thousand.

★ Dr Jacques Locard of France invented the breathalyser in 1952, but died before he was able to patent the invention.

★ Frank Williams, famous for the Williams Formula One and Grand Prix cars, began producing Formula One cars in 1969.

★ The Newman-Haas Indy Car racing team was begun in the United States in 1983 by the actor Paul Newman and Cecil Haas. Nigel Mansell, the British winner of the world motor racing championships, joined the team in a £3 million deal in 1992. Mansell went

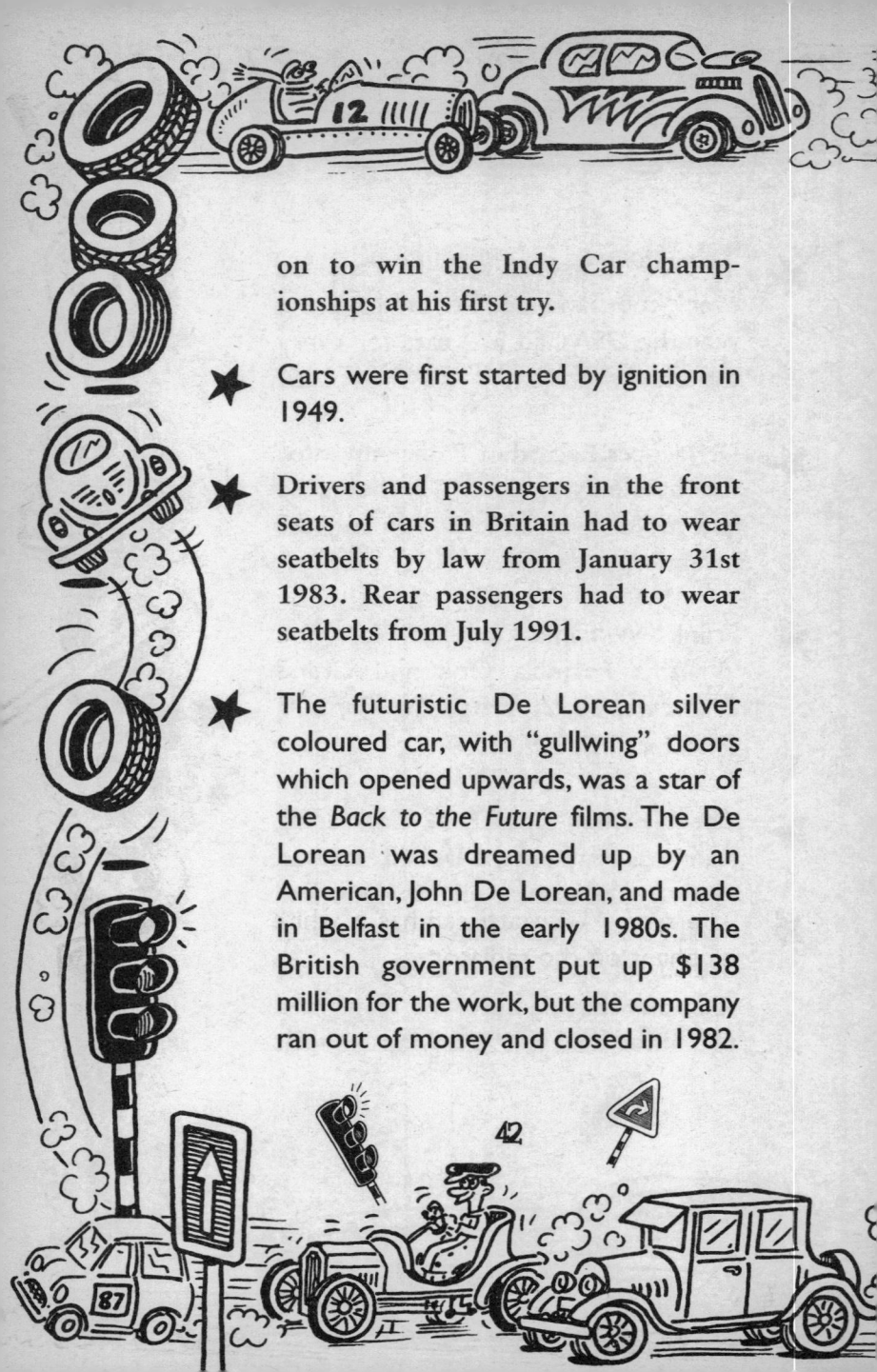

on to win the Indy Car championships at his first try.

★ Cars were first started by ignition in
1949.

★ Drivers and passengers in the front
seats of cars in Britain had to wear
seatbelts by law from January 31st
1983. Rear passengers had to wear
seatbelts from July 1991.

★ The futuristic De Lorean silver
coloured car, with "gullwing" doors
which opened upwards, was a star of
the *Back to the Future* films. The De
Lorean was dreamed up by an
American, John De Lorean, and made
in Belfast in the early 1980s. The
British government put up $138
million for the work, but the company
ran out of money and closed in 1982.

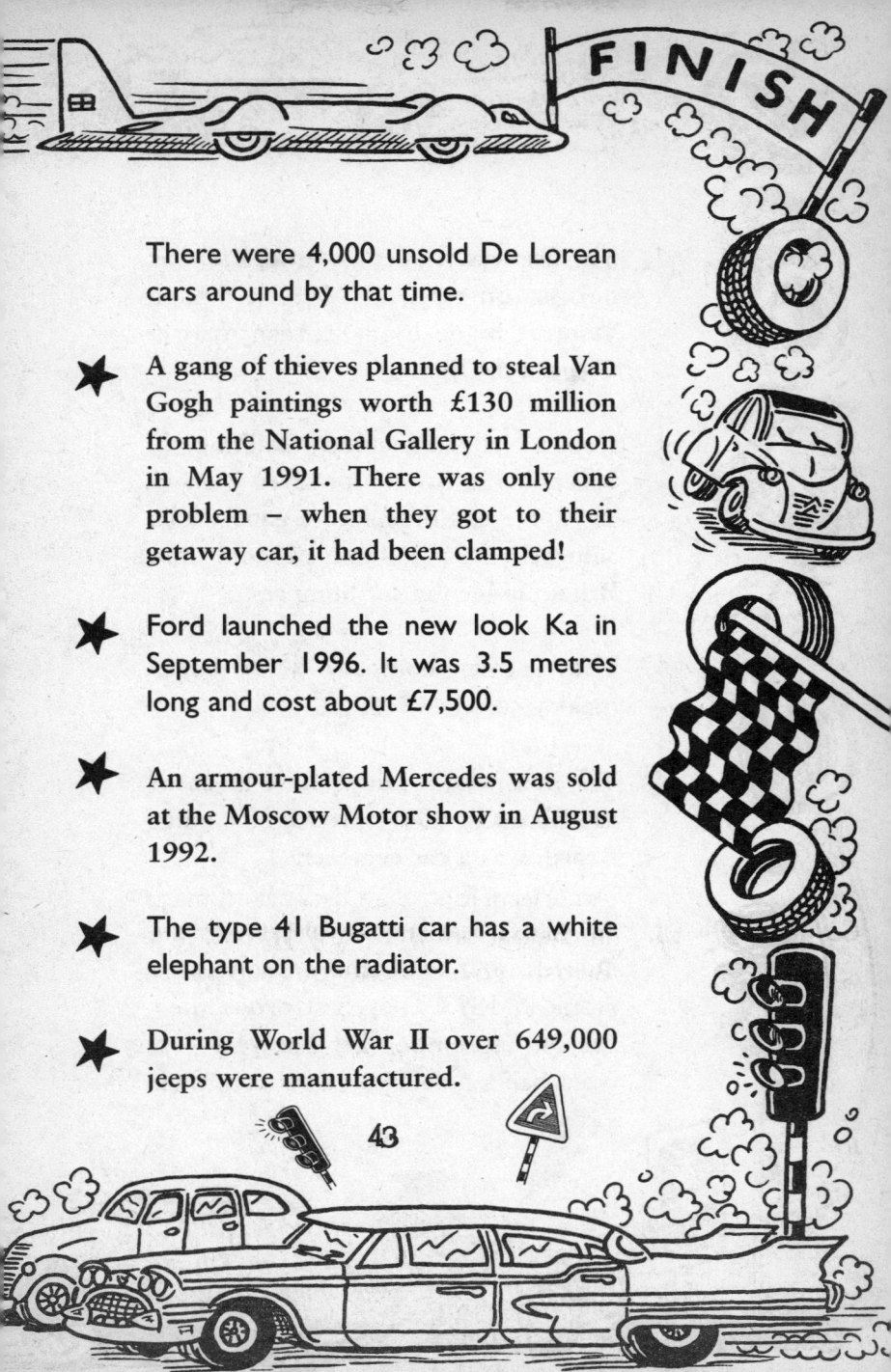

There were 4,000 unsold De Lorean cars around by that time.

★ A gang of thieves planned to steal Van Gogh paintings worth £130 million from the National Gallery in London in May 1991. There was only one problem – when they got to their getaway car, it had been clamped!

★ Ford launched the new look Ka in September 1996. It was 3.5 metres long and cost about £7,500.

★ An armour-plated Mercedes was sold at the Moscow Motor show in August 1992.

★ The type 41 Bugatti car has a white elephant on the radiator.

★ During World War II over 649,000 jeeps were manufactured.

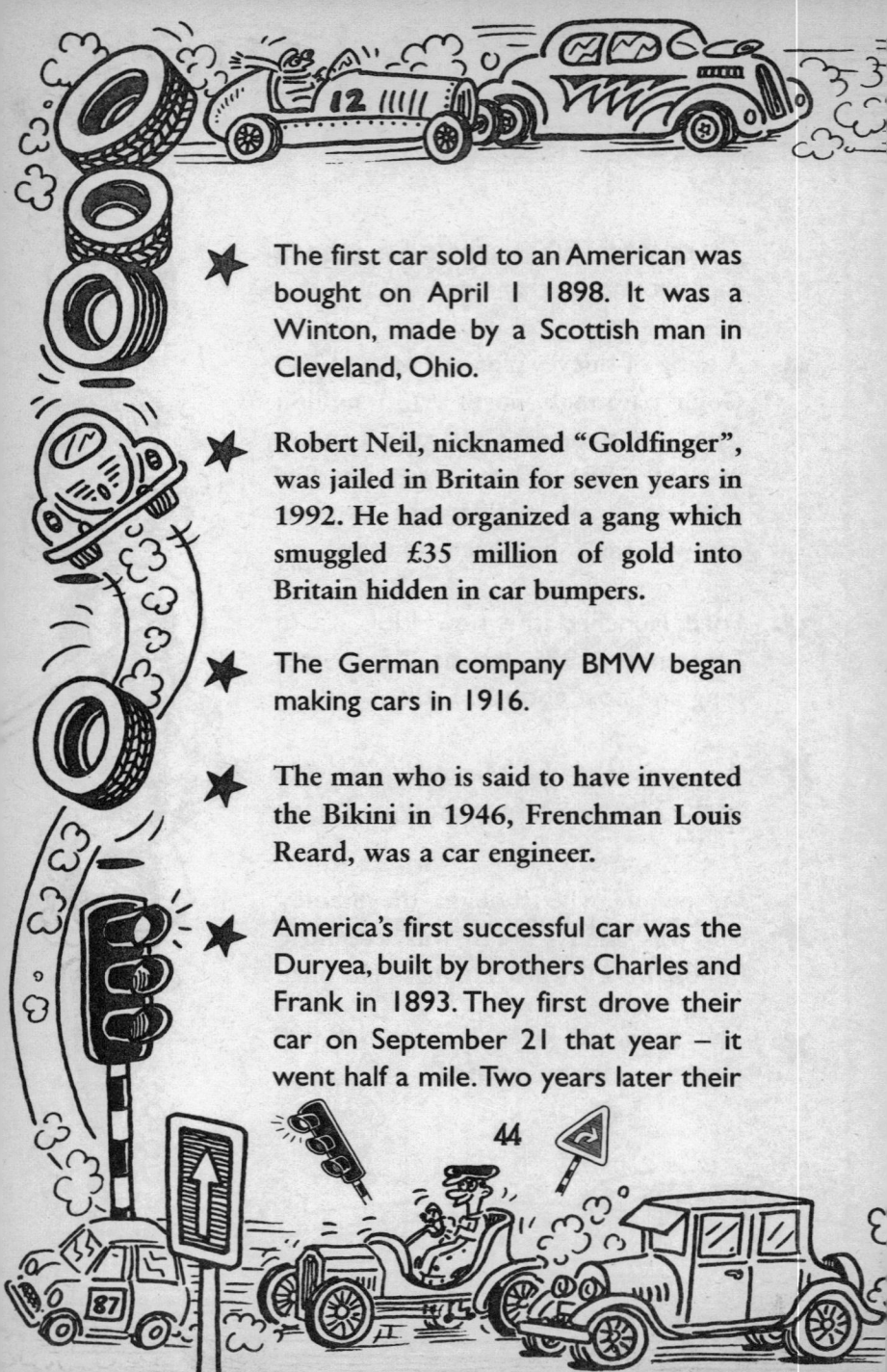

The first car sold to an American was bought on April 1 1898. It was a Winton, made by a Scottish man in Cleveland, Ohio.

Robert Neil, nicknamed "Goldfinger", was jailed in Britain for seven years in 1992. He had organized a gang which smuggled £35 million of gold into Britain hidden in car bumpers.

The German company BMW began making cars in 1916.

The man who is said to have invented the Bikini in 1946, Frenchman Louis Reard, was a car engineer.

America's first successful car was the Duryea, built by brothers Charles and Frank in 1893. They first drove their car on September 21 that year – it went half a mile. Two years later their

44

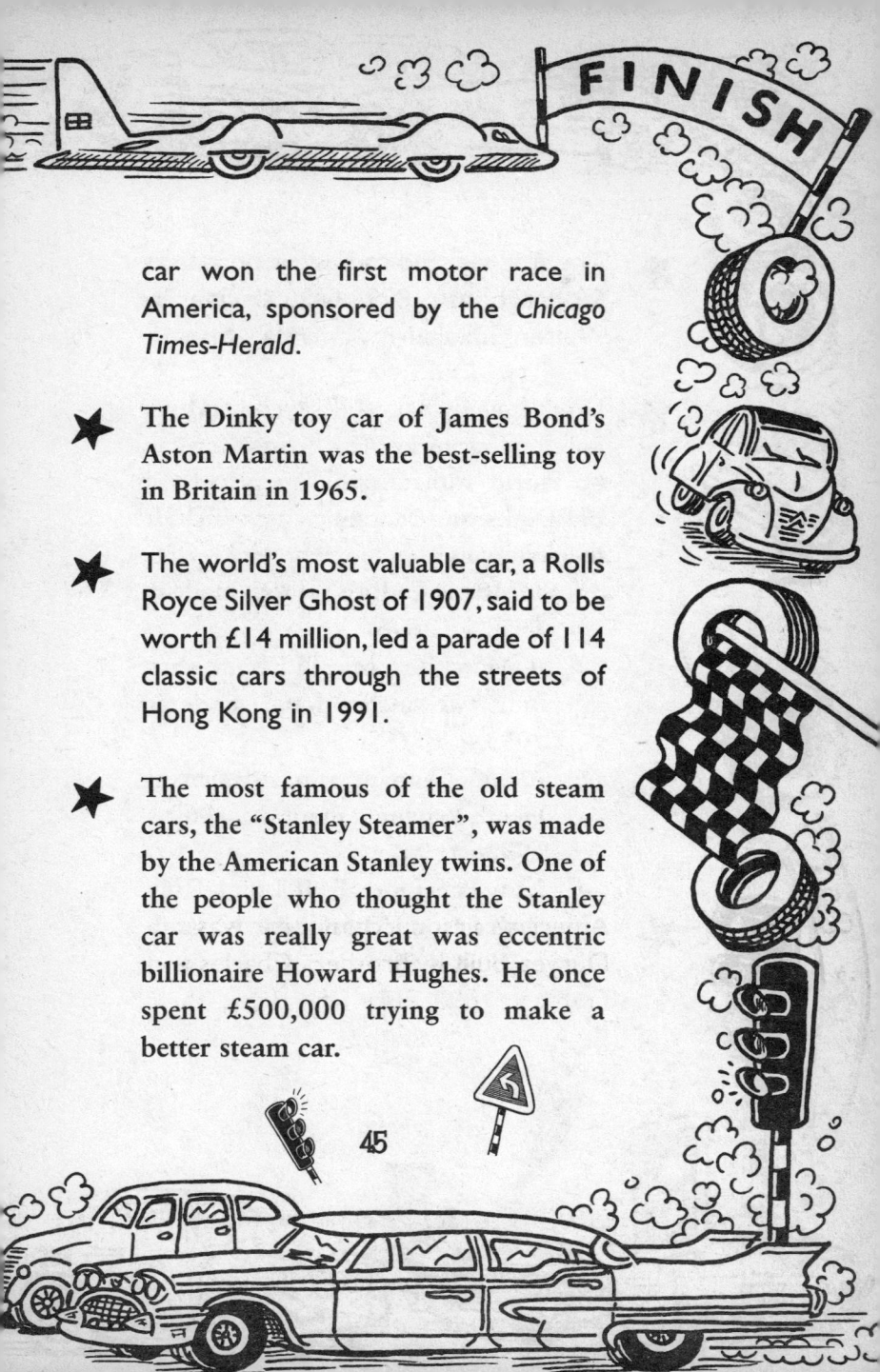

car won the first motor race in America, sponsored by the *Chicago Times-Herald*.

★ The Dinky toy car of James Bond's Aston Martin was the best-selling toy in Britain in 1965.

★ The world's most valuable car, a Rolls Royce Silver Ghost of 1907, said to be worth £14 million, led a parade of 114 classic cars through the streets of Hong Kong in 1991.

★ The most famous of the old steam cars, the "Stanley Steamer", was made by the American Stanley twins. One of the people who thought the Stanley car was really great was eccentric billionaire Howard Hughes. He once spent £500,000 trying to make a better steam car.

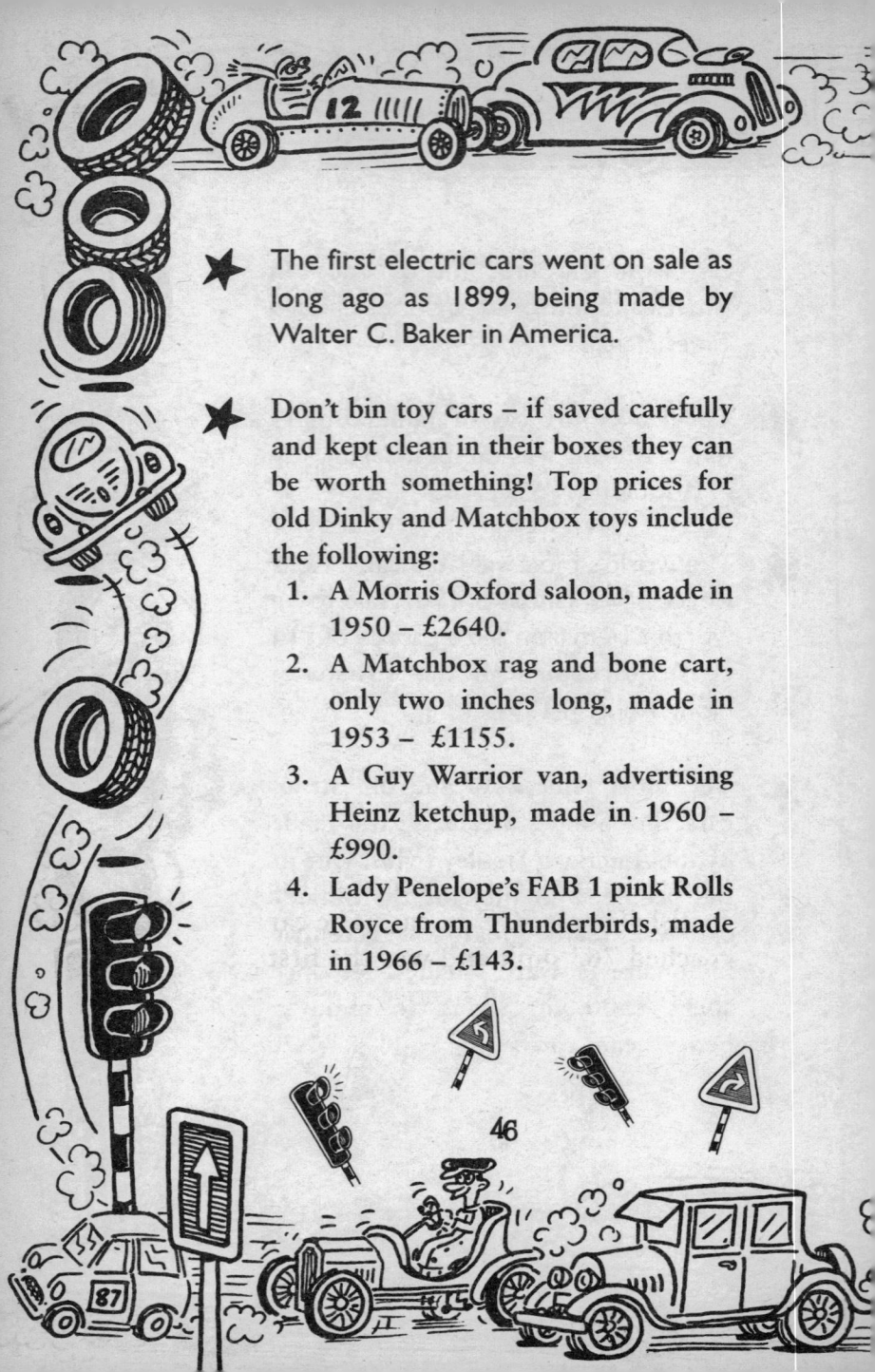

★ The first electric cars went on sale as long ago as 1899, being made by Walter C. Baker in America.

★ Don't bin toy cars – if saved carefully and kept clean in their boxes they can be worth something! Top prices for old Dinky and Matchbox toys include the following:

1. A Morris Oxford saloon, made in 1950 – £2640.

2. A Matchbox rag and bone cart, only two inches long, made in 1953 – £1155.

3. A Guy Warrior van, advertising Heinz ketchup, made in 1960 – £990.

4. Lady Penelope's FAB 1 pink Rolls Royce from Thunderbirds, made in 1966 – £143.

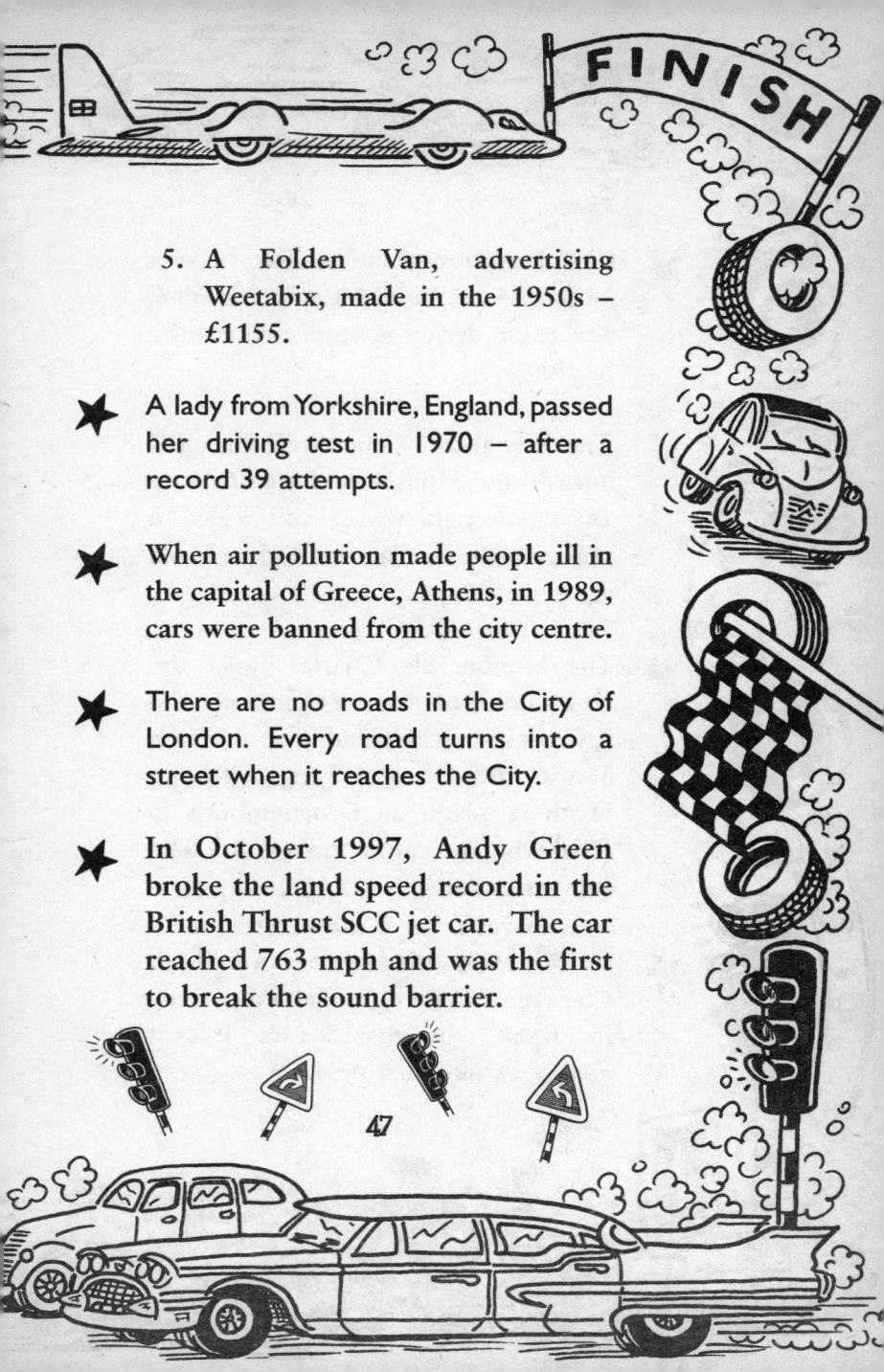

5. A Folden Van, advertising Weetabix, made in the 1950s – £1155.

★ A lady from Yorkshire, England, passed her driving test in 1970 – after a record 39 attempts.

★ When air pollution made people ill in the capital of Greece, Athens, in 1989, cars were banned from the city centre.

★ There are no roads in the City of London. Every road turns into a street when it reaches the City.

★ In October 1997, Andy Green broke the land speed record in the British Thrust SCC jet car. The car reached 763 mph and was the first to break the sound barrier.

47

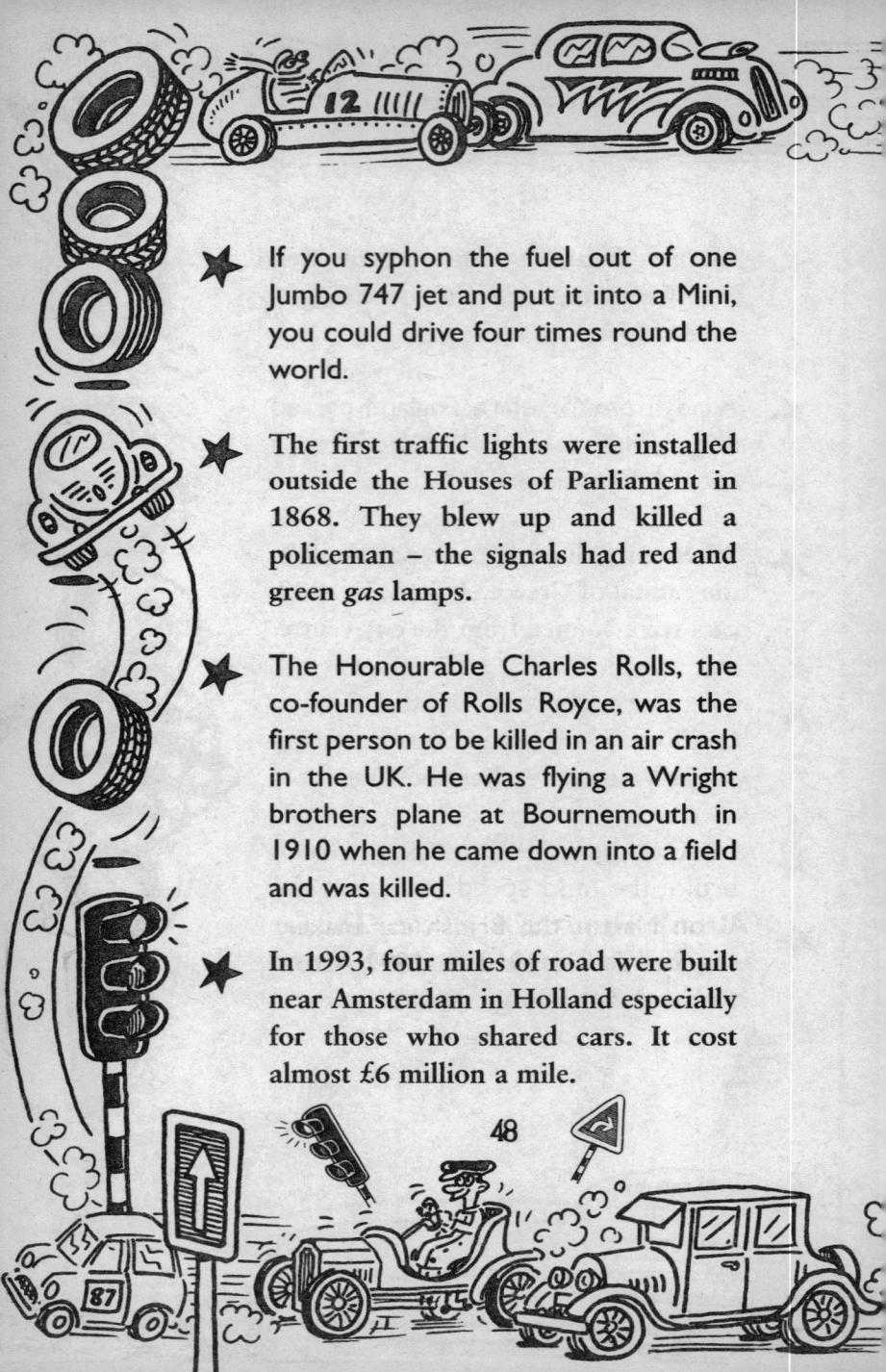

★ If you syphon the fuel out of one Jumbo 747 jet and put it into a Mini, you could drive four times round the world.

★ The first traffic lights were installed outside the Houses of Parliament in 1868. They blew up and killed a policeman – the signals had red and green *gas* lamps.

★ The Honourable Charles Rolls, the co-founder of Rolls Royce, was the first person to be killed in an air crash in the UK. He was flying a Wright brothers plane at Bournemouth in 1910 when he came down into a field and was killed.

★ In 1993, four miles of road were built near Amsterdam in Holland especially for those who shared cars. It cost almost £6 million a mile.

48

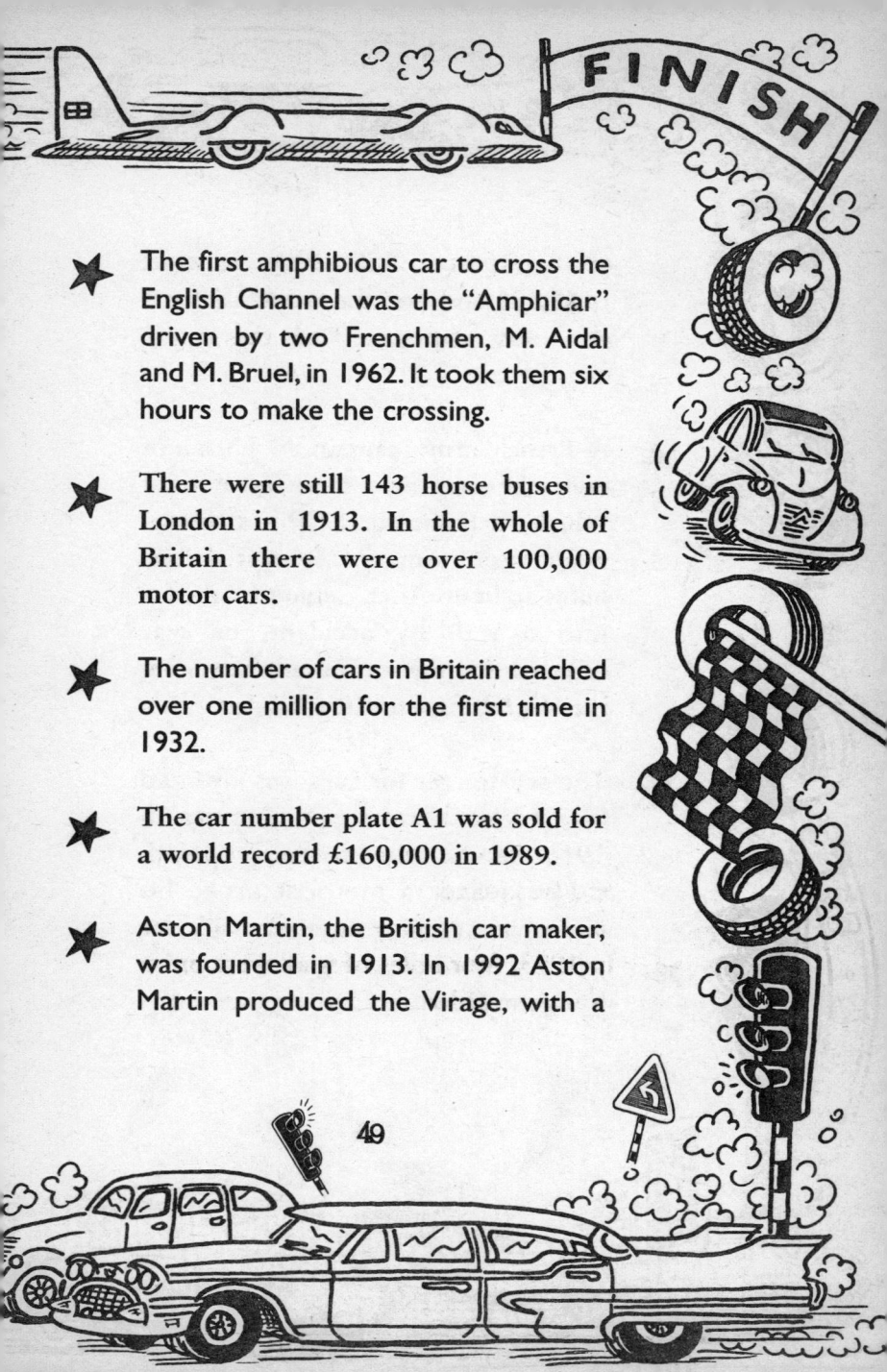

★ The first amphibious car to cross the English Channel was the "Amphicar" driven by two Frenchmen, M. Aidal and M. Bruel, in 1962. It took them six hours to make the crossing.

★ There were still 143 horse buses in London in 1913. In the whole of Britain there were over 100,000 motor cars.

★ The number of cars in Britain reached over one million for the first time in 1932.

★ The car number plate A1 was sold for a world record £160,000 in 1989.

★ Aston Martin, the British car maker, was founded in 1913. In 1992 Aston Martin produced the Virage, with a

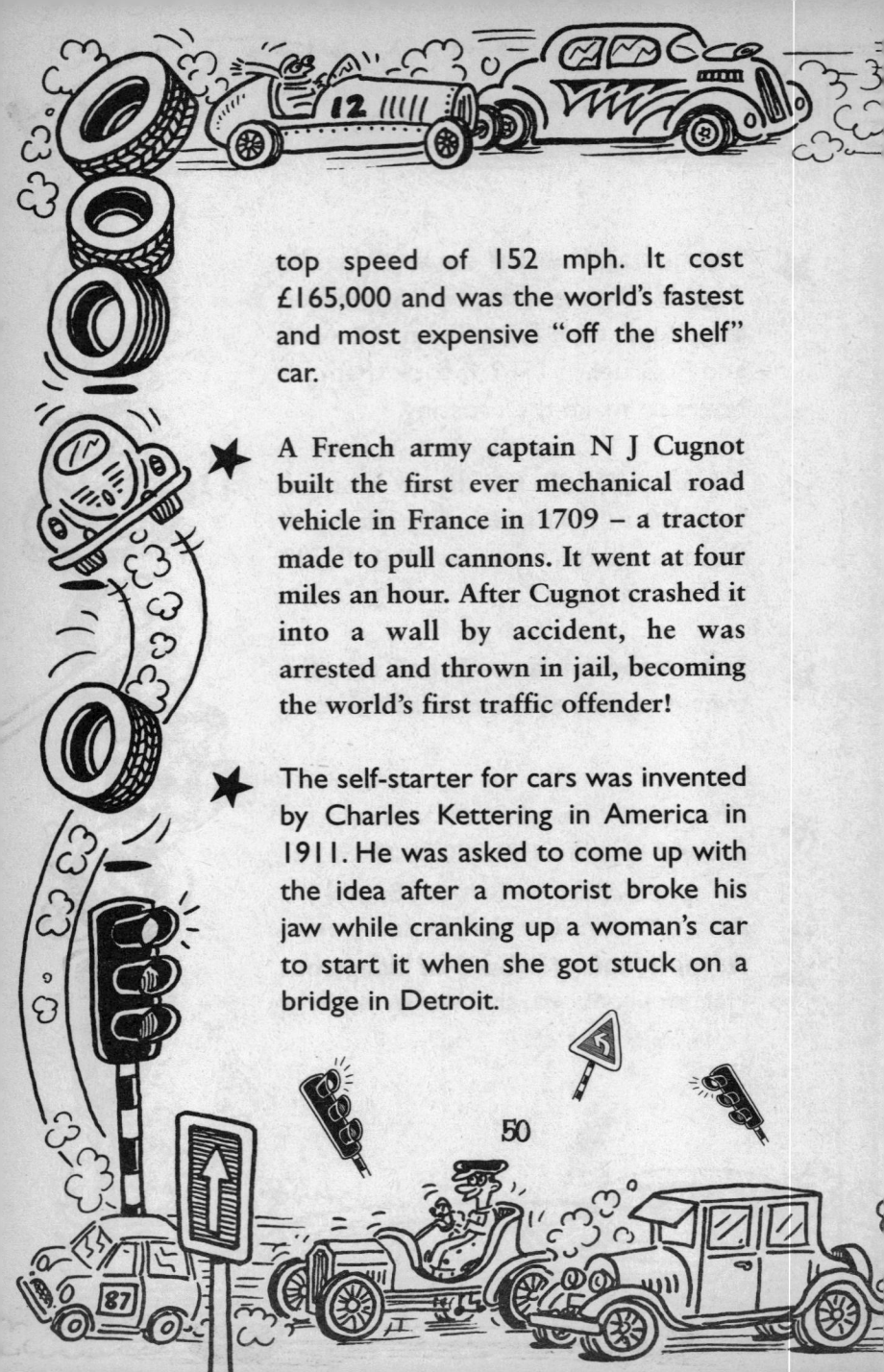

top speed of 152 mph. It cost £165,000 and was the world's fastest and most expensive "off the shelf" car.

★ A French army captain N J Cugnot built the first ever mechanical road vehicle in France in 1709 – a tractor made to pull cannons. It went at four miles an hour. After Cugnot crashed it into a wall by accident, he was arrested and thrown in jail, becoming the world's first traffic offender!

★ The self-starter for cars was invented by Charles Kettering in America in 1911. He was asked to come up with the idea after a motorist broke his jaw while cranking up a woman's car to start it when she got stuck on a bridge in Detroit.

50

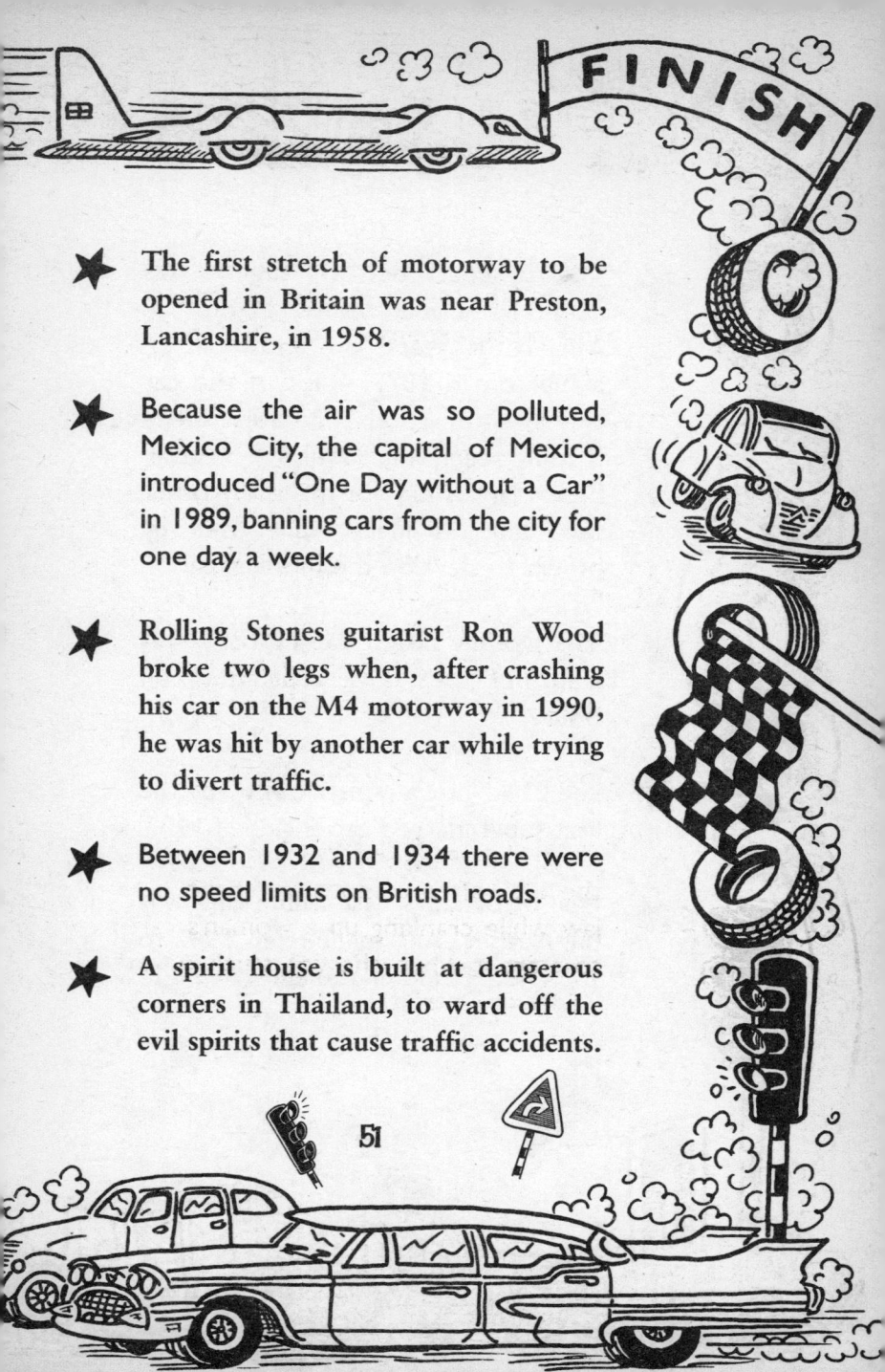

★ The first stretch of motorway to be opened in Britain was near Preston, Lancashire, in 1958.

★ Because the air was so polluted, Mexico City, the capital of Mexico, introduced "One Day without a Car" in 1989, banning cars from the city for one day a week.

★ Rolling Stones guitarist Ron Wood broke two legs when, after crashing his car on the M4 motorway in 1990, he was hit by another car while trying to divert traffic.

★ Between 1932 and 1934 there were no speed limits on British roads.

★ A spirit house is built at dangerous corners in Thailand, to ward off the evil spirits that cause traffic accidents.

51

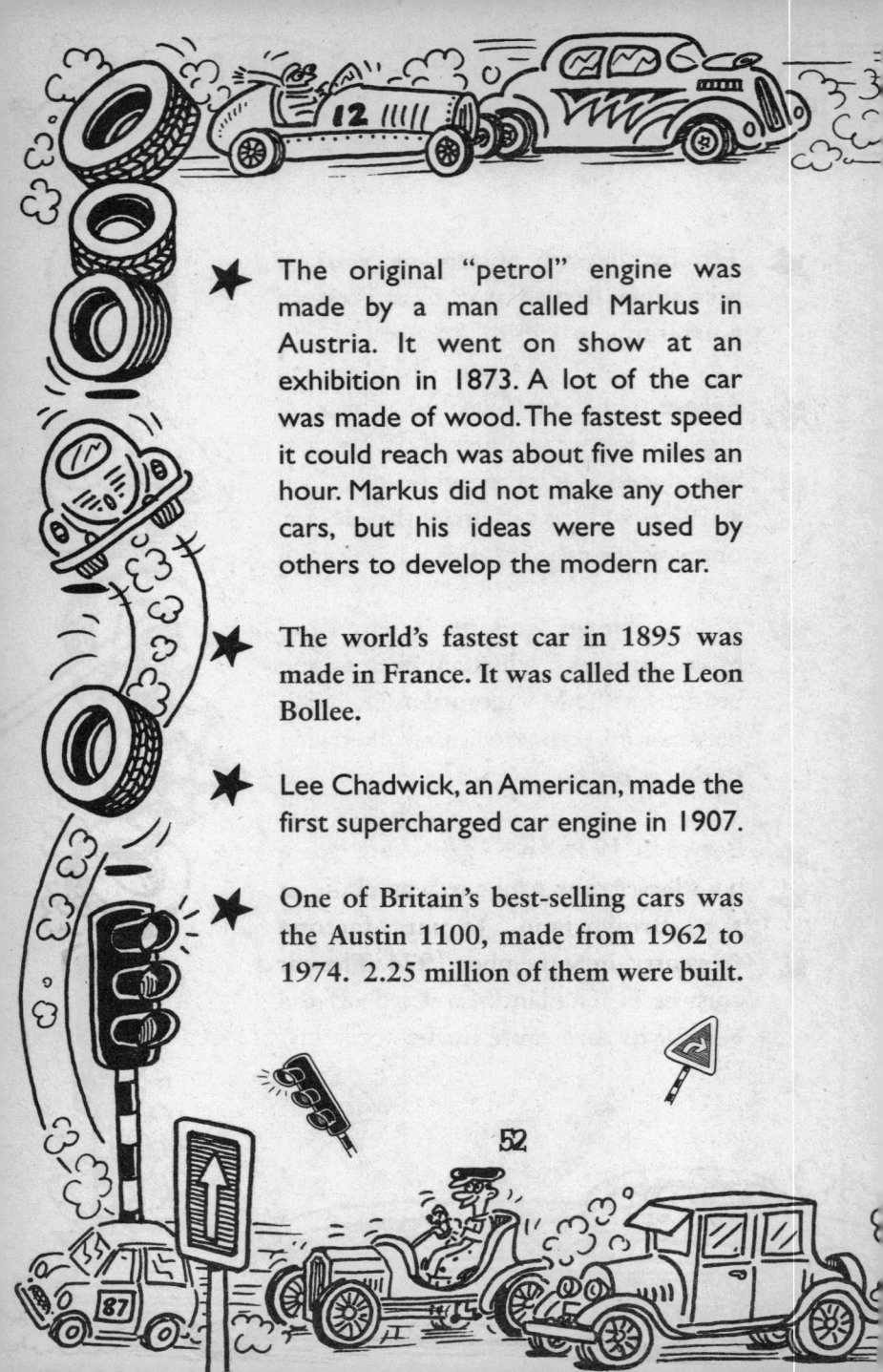

★ The original "petrol" engine was made by a man called Markus in Austria. It went on show at an exhibition in 1873. A lot of the car was made of wood. The fastest speed it could reach was about five miles an hour. Markus did not make any other cars, but his ideas were used by others to develop the modern car.

★ The world's fastest car in 1895 was made in France. It was called the Leon Bollee.

★ Lee Chadwick, an American, made the first supercharged car engine in 1907.

★ One of Britain's best-selling cars was the Austin 1100, made from 1962 to 1974. 2.25 million of them were built.

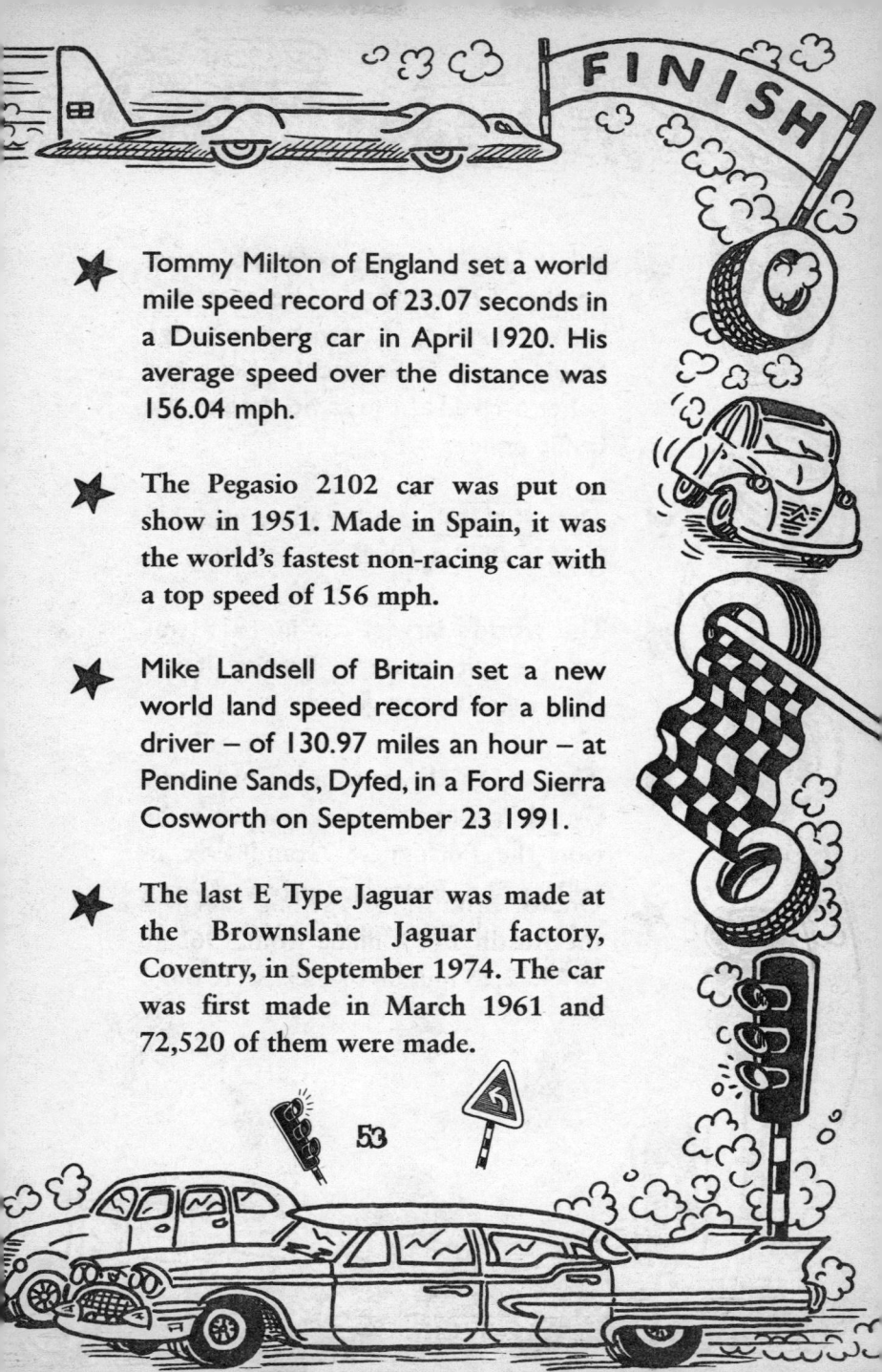

★ Tommy Milton of England set a world mile speed record of 23.07 seconds in a Duisenberg car in April 1920. His average speed over the distance was 156.04 mph.

★ The Pegasio 2102 car was put on show in 1951. Made in Spain, it was the world's fastest non-racing car with a top speed of 156 mph.

★ Mike Landsell of Britain set a new world land speed record for a blind driver – of 130.97 miles an hour – at Pendine Sands, Dyfed, in a Ford Sierra Cosworth on September 23 1991.

★ The last E Type Jaguar was made at the Brownslane Jaguar factory, Coventry, in September 1974. The car was first made in March 1961 and 72,520 of them were made.

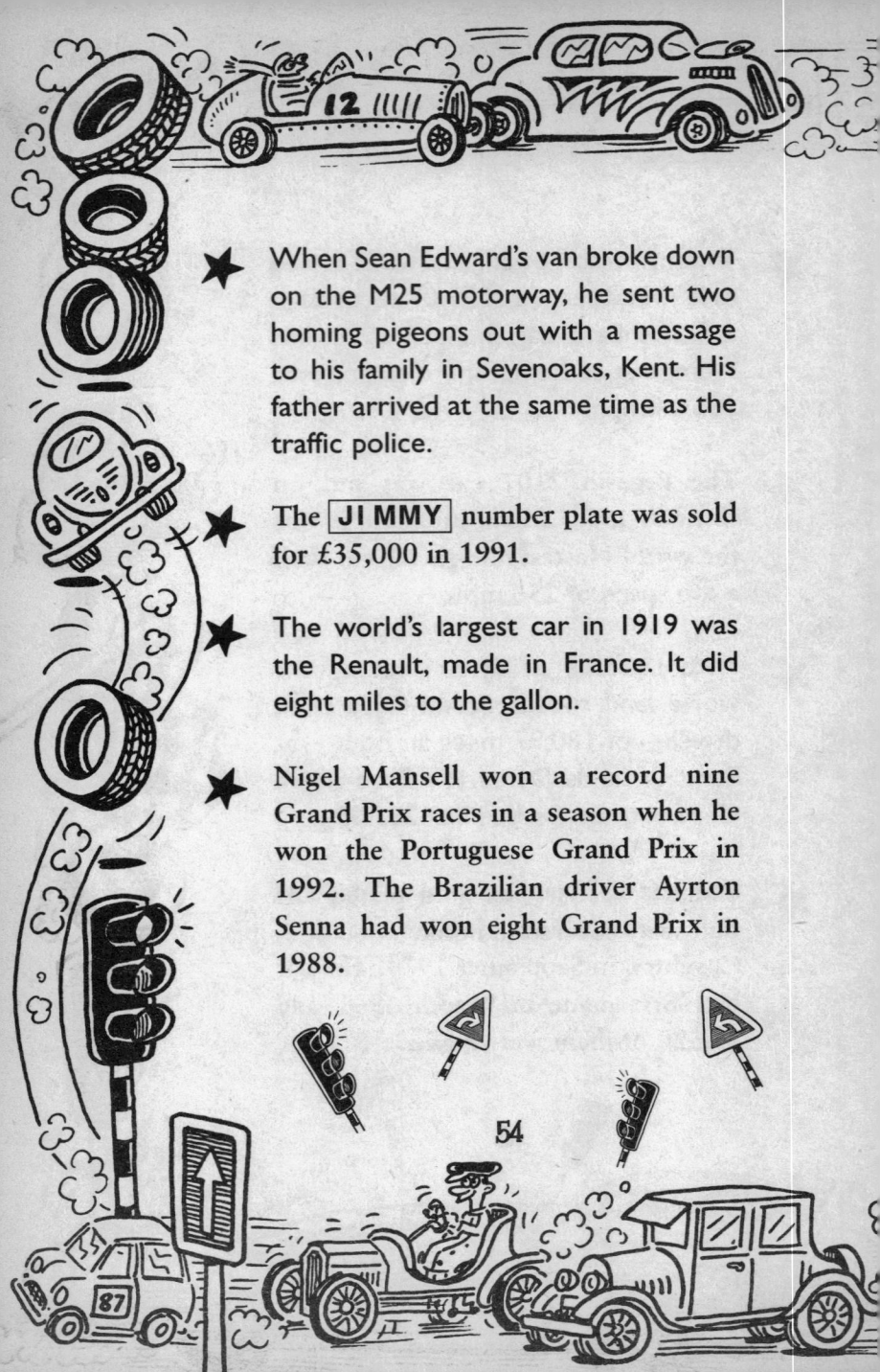

★ When Sean Edward's van broke down on the M25 motorway, he sent two homing pigeons out with a message to his family in Sevenoaks, Kent. His father arrived at the same time as the traffic police.

★ The JI MMY number plate was sold for £35,000 in 1991.

★ The world's largest car in 1919 was the Renault, made in France. It did eight miles to the gallon.

★ Nigel Mansell won a record nine Grand Prix races in a season when he won the Portuguese Grand Prix in 1992. The Brazilian driver Ayrton Senna had won eight Grand Prix in 1988.

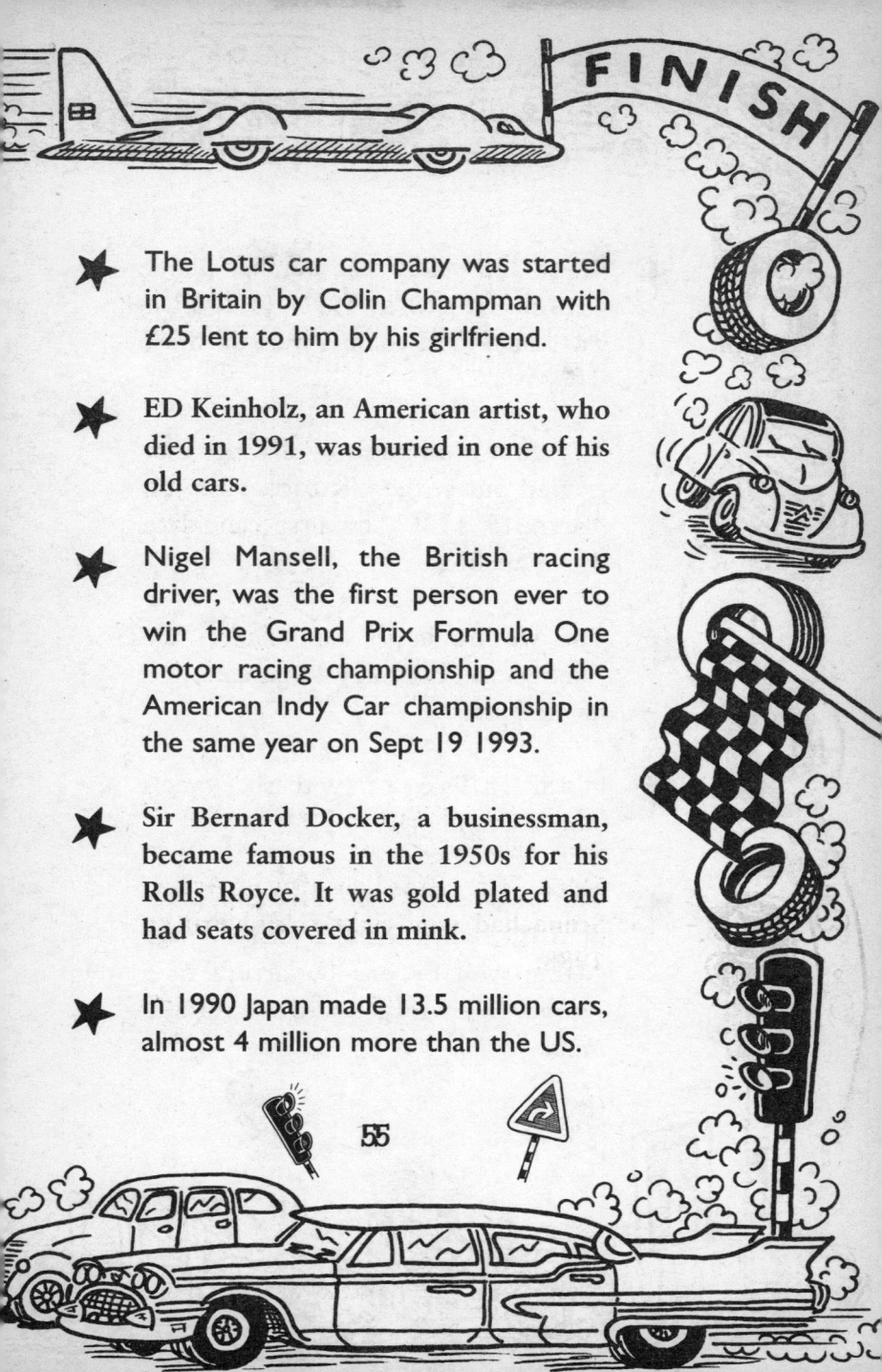

FINISH

★ The Lotus car company was started in Britain by Colin Champman with £25 lent to him by his girlfriend.

★ ED Keinholz, an American artist, who died in 1991, was buried in one of his old cars.

★ Nigel Mansell, the British racing driver, was the first person ever to win the Grand Prix Formula One motor racing championship and the American Indy Car championship in the same year on Sept 19 1993.

★ Sir Bernard Docker, a businessman, became famous in the 1950s for his Rolls Royce. It was gold plated and had seats covered in mink.

★ In 1990 Japan made 13.5 million cars, almost 4 million more than the US.

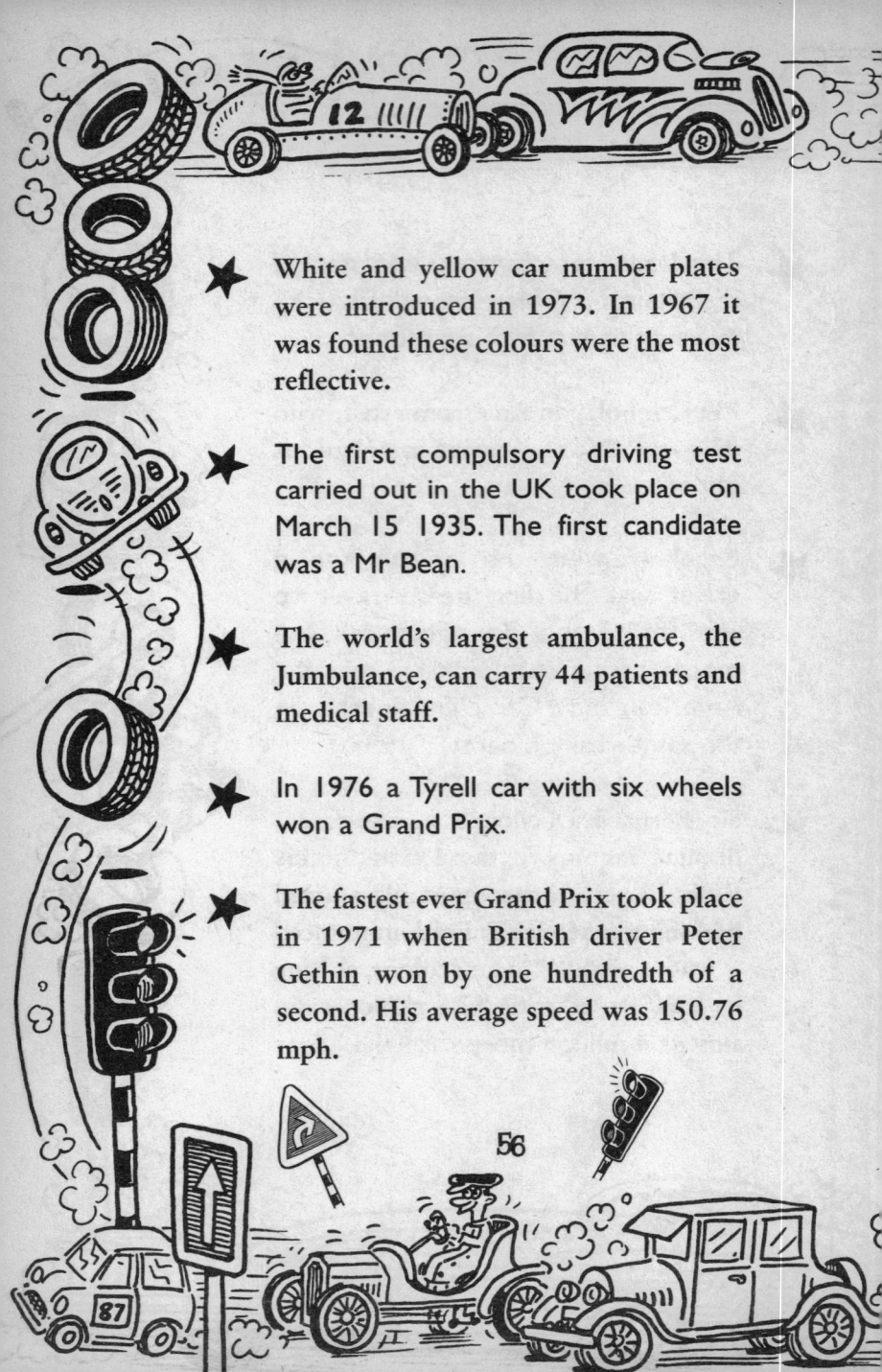

★ White and yellow car number plates were introduced in 1973. In 1967 it was found these colours were the most reflective.

★ The first compulsory driving test carried out in the UK took place on March 15 1935. The first candidate was a Mr Bean.

★ The world's largest ambulance, the Jumbulance, can carry 44 patients and medical staff.

★ In 1976 a Tyrell car with six wheels won a Grand Prix.

★ The fastest ever Grand Prix took place in 1971 when British driver Peter Gethin won by one hundredth of a second. His average speed was 150.76 mph.

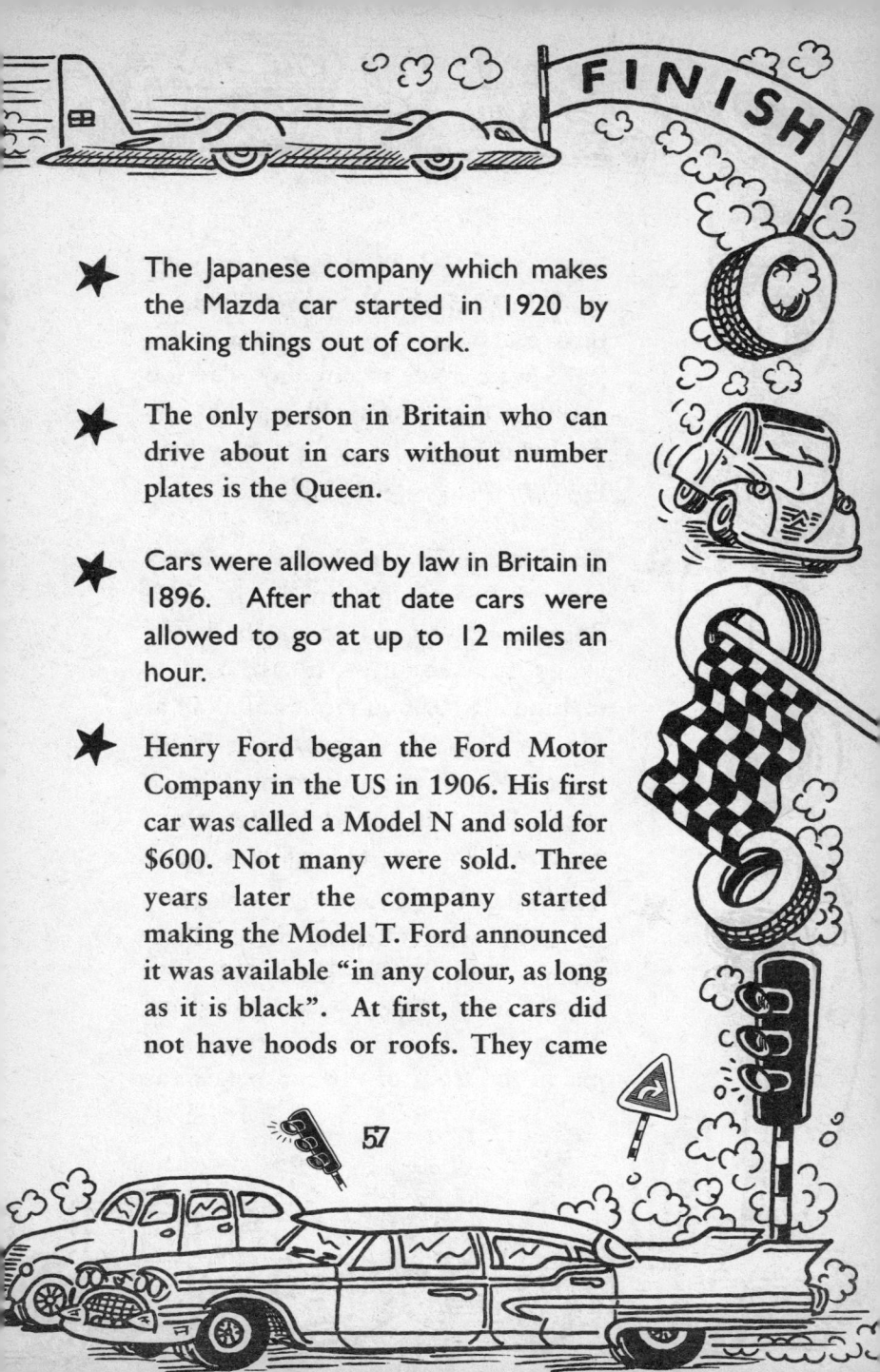

★ The Japanese company which makes the Mazda car started in 1920 by making things out of cork.

★ The only person in Britain who can drive about in cars without number plates is the Queen.

★ Cars were allowed by law in Britain in 1896. After that date cars were allowed to go at up to 12 miles an hour.

★ Henry Ford began the Ford Motor Company in the US in 1906. His first car was called a Model N and sold for $600. Not many were sold. Three years later the company started making the Model T. Ford announced it was available "in any colour, as long as it is black". At first, the cars did not have hoods or roofs. They came

57

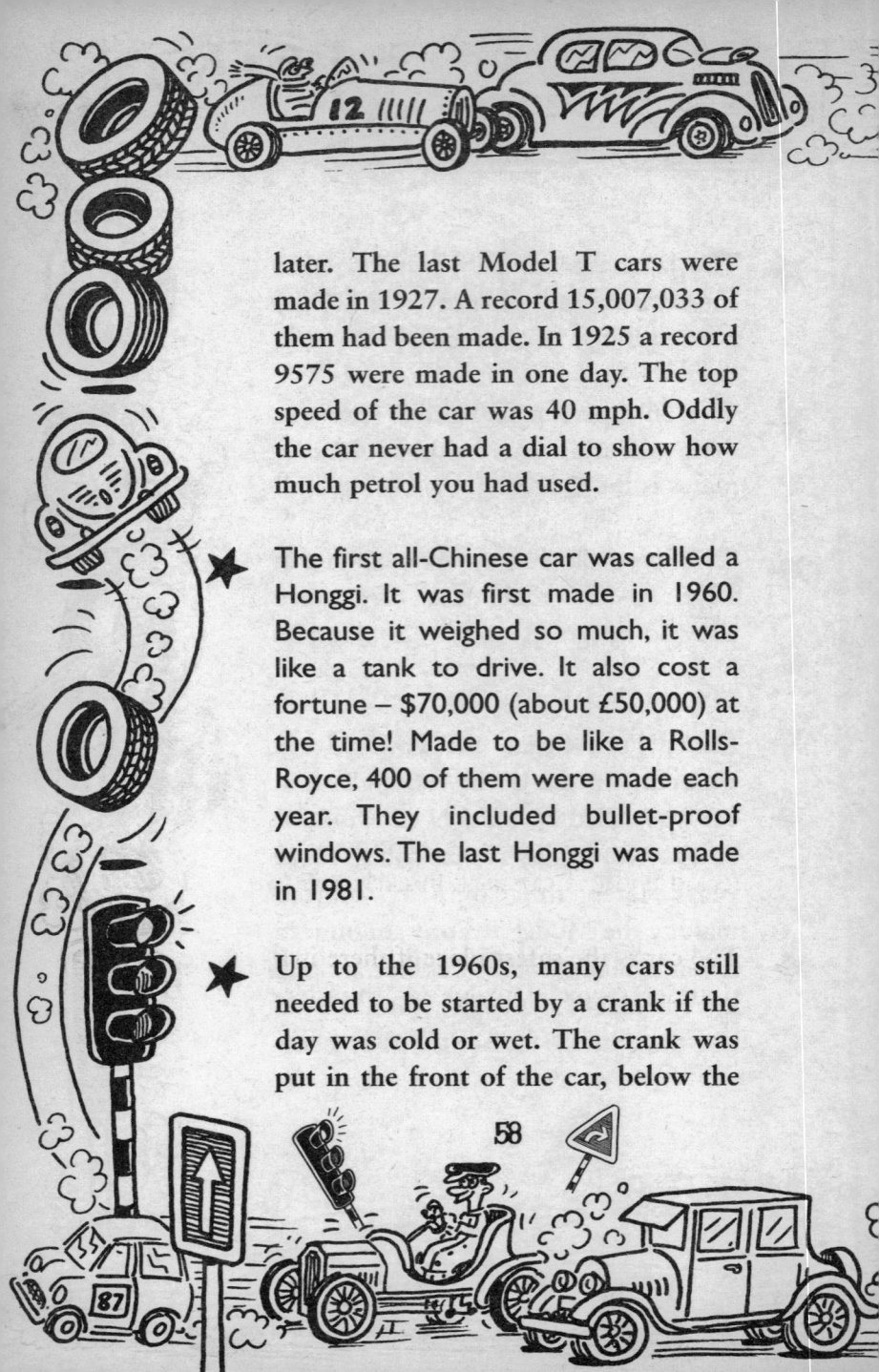

later. The last Model T cars were made in 1927. A record 15,007,033 of them had been made. In 1925 a record 9575 were made in one day. The top speed of the car was 40 mph. Oddly the car never had a dial to show how much petrol you had used.

The first all-Chinese car was called a Honggi. It was first made in 1960. Because it weighed so much, it was like a tank to drive. It also cost a fortune – $70,000 (about £50,000) at the time! Made to be like a Rolls-Royce, 400 of them were made each year. They included bullet-proof windows. The last Honggi was made in 1981.

Up to the 1960s, many cars still needed to be started by a crank if the day was cold or wet. The crank was put in the front of the car, below the

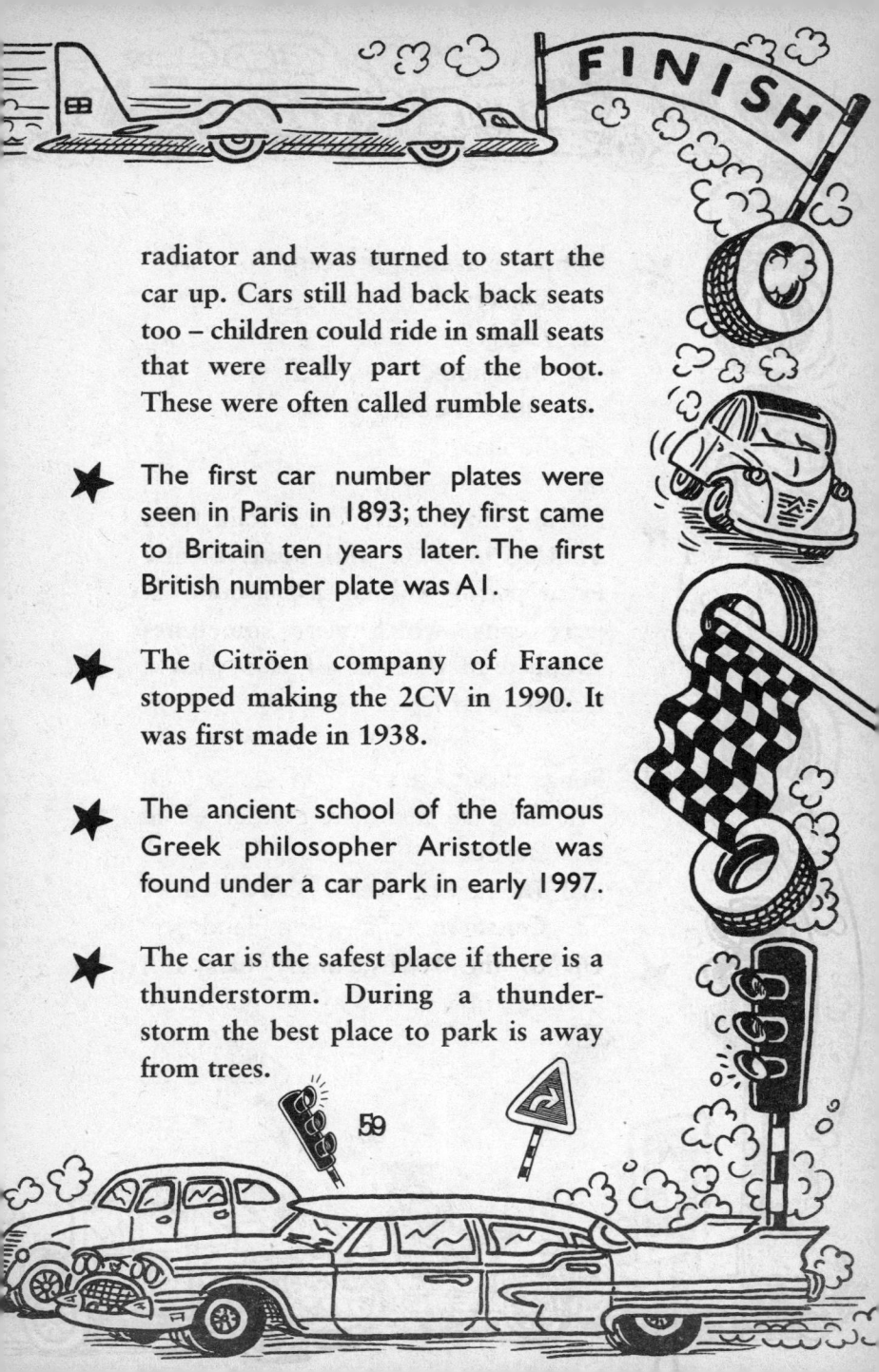

radiator and was turned to start the car up. Cars still had back back seats too – children could ride in small seats that were really part of the boot. These were often called rumble seats.

★ The first car number plates were seen in Paris in 1893; they first came to Britain ten years later. The first British number plate was A1.

★ The Citröen company of France stopped making the 2CV in 1990. It was first made in 1938.

★ The ancient school of the famous Greek philosopher Aristotle was found under a car park in early 1997.

★ The car is the safest place if there is a thunderstorm. During a thunderstorm the best place to park is away from trees.

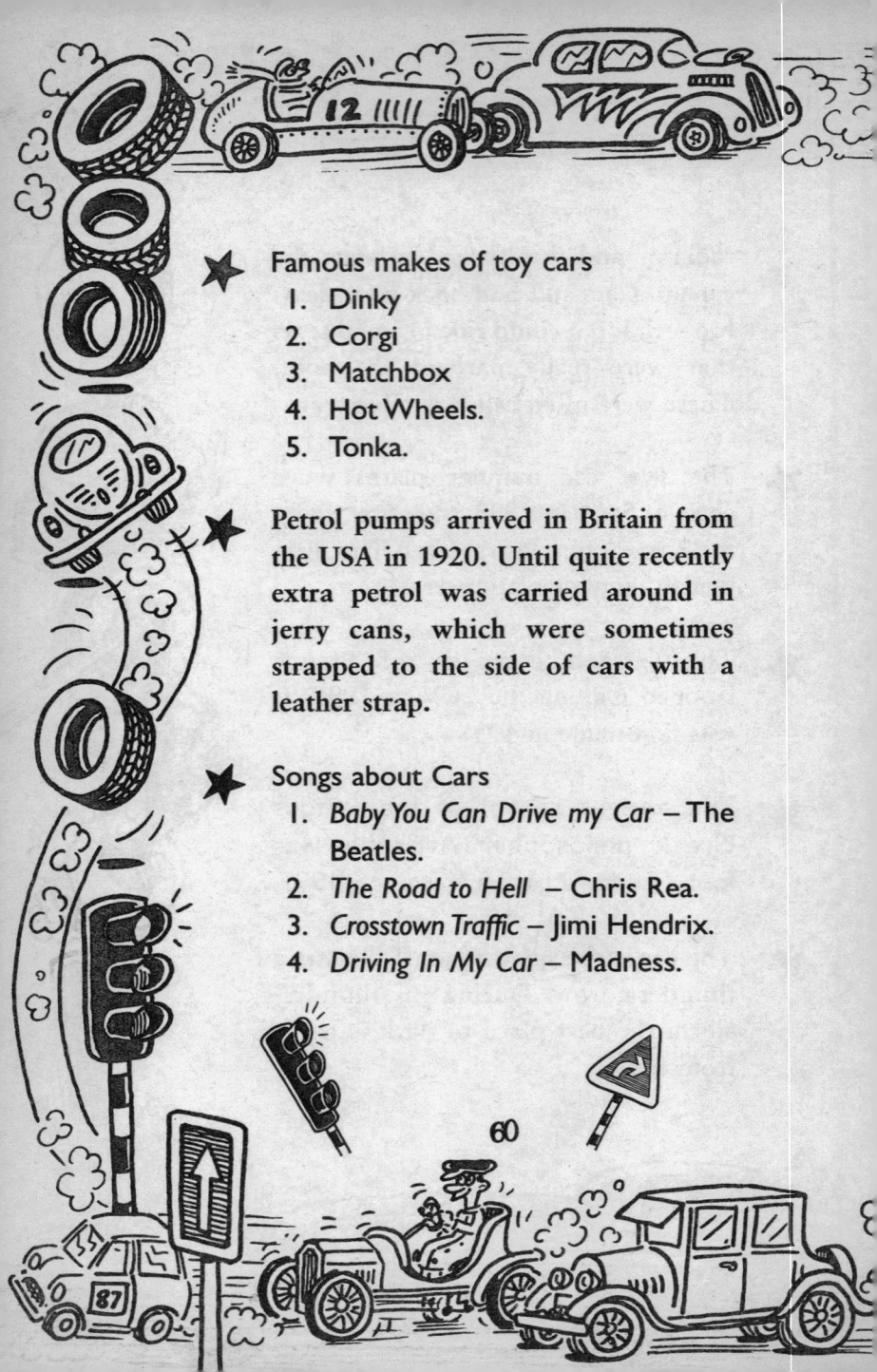

★ Famous makes of toy cars
1. Dinky
2. Corgi
3. Matchbox
4. Hot Wheels.
5. Tonka.

★ Petrol pumps arrived in Britain from the USA in 1920. Until quite recently extra petrol was carried around in jerry cans, which were sometimes strapped to the side of cars with a leather strap.

★ Songs about Cars
1. *Baby You Can Drive my Car* – The Beatles.
2. *The Road to Hell* – Chris Rea.
3. *Crosstown Traffic* – Jimi Hendrix.
4. *Driving In My Car* – Madness.

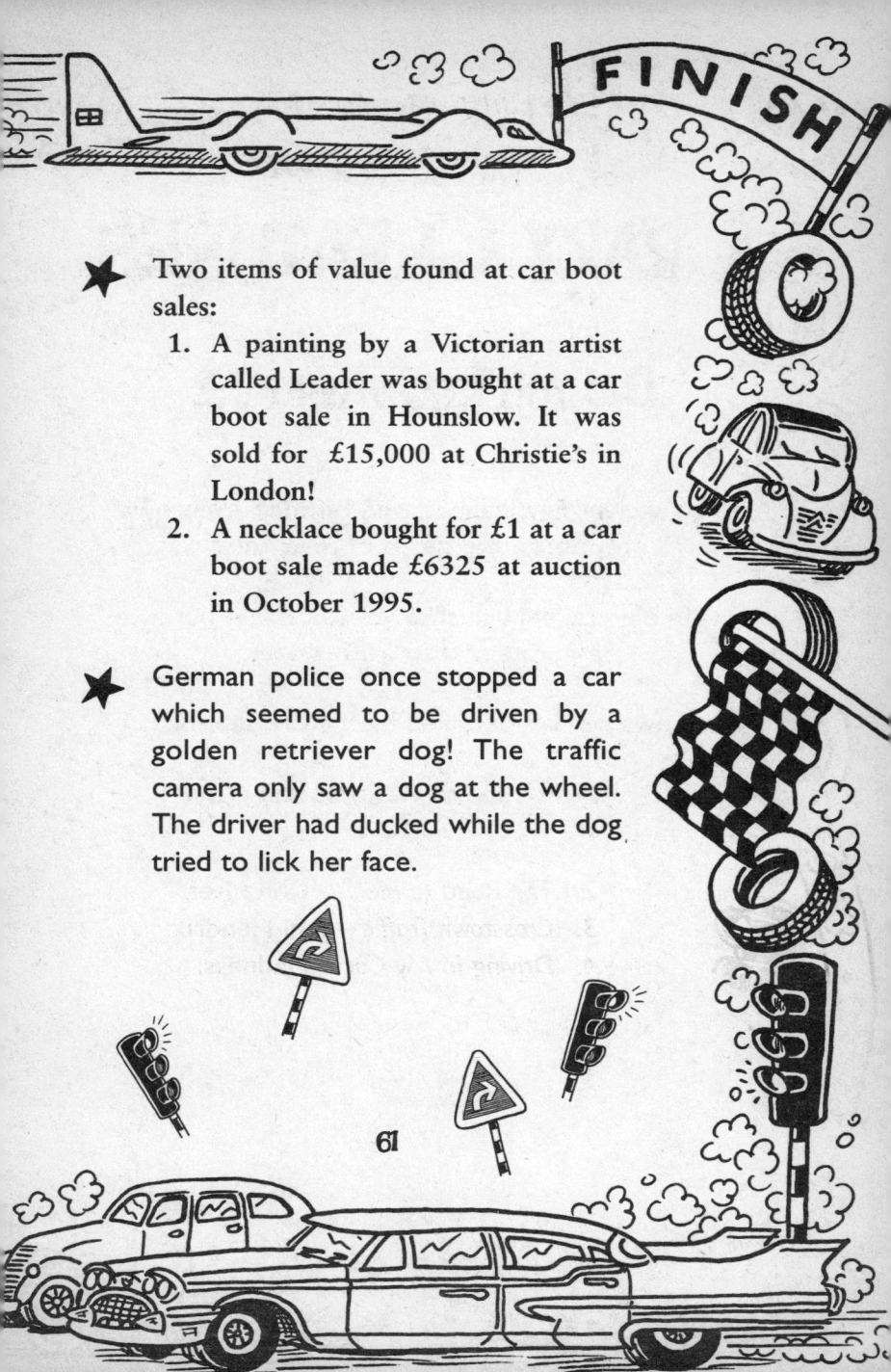

★ Two items of value found at car boot sales:

1. A painting by a Victorian artist called Leader was bought at a car boot sale in Hounslow. It was sold for £15,000 at Christie's in London!

2. A necklace bought for £1 at a car boot sale made £6325 at auction in October 1995.

★ German police once stopped a car which seemed to be driven by a golden retriever dog! The traffic camera only saw a dog at the wheel. The driver had ducked while the dog tried to lick her face.

FACT ATTACK

CRAZY CREATURES

DID YOU KNOW THAT . . .

The ancient Egyptians shaved off their eyebrows
to mourn the death of their cats.

An electric eel will short-circuit if it is put in
salt, rather than fresh, water.

Cows can be identified by their noseprints.

Jellyfish sometimes evaporate.

Also published by Macmillan

FACT ATTACK

FANTASTIC FOOTBALL

DID YOU KNOW THAT . . .

James I of England was probably the first king to attend a game of football.

In the 1966 World Cup final, Geoff Hurst scored three goals – one with a header, one with his left foot and one with his right foot!

Fact Attack titles available from Macmillan

The prices shown below are correct at the time of going to press.
However, Macmillan Publishers reserve the right to show new retail prices
on covers which may differ from those previously advertised.

Awesome Aliens	**Ian Locke**	**£1.99**
Beastly Bodies	**Ian Locke**	**£1.99**
Crazy Creatures	**Ian Locke**	**£1.99**
Fantastic Football	**Ian Locke**	**£1.99**
Dastardly Deeds	**Ian Locke**	**£1.99**
Cool Cars	**Ian Locke**	**£1.99**
Mad Medicine	**Ian Locke**	**£1.99**
Gruesome Ghosts	**Ian Locke**	**£1.99**
Dreadful Disasters	**Ian Locke**	**£1.99**
Nutty Numbers	**Rowland Morgan**	**£1.99**

All Macmillan titles can be ordered at your local bookshop
or are available by post from:

**Book Service by Post
PO Box 29, Douglas, Isle of Man IM99 1BQ**

Credit cards accepted. For details:
Telephone: 01624 675137
Fax: 01624 670923
E-mail: bookshop@enterprise.net

Free postage and packing in the UK.
Overseas customers: add £1 per book (paperback)
and £3 per book (hardback).